365

Days of

SLOW-COOKING

Design copyrighted 2012 by Covenant Communications, Inc.
American Fork, Utah

Copyright 2012 by Karen Bellessa Petersen
Photos on pages 39, 70, 74, 76, 118, 131, 141, 184 and second photo from the left on the back cover by Katie Dudley. www.katiedudleyphotography.com
All other images © iStockphoto.com
Cover and book design by Jennie Williams, © 2012 Covenant Communications, Inc.

Printed in China
First Printing March 2012

22 21 20 19 18 17 16   10 9 8 7 6 5 4 3 2 1

ISBN: 978-1-52440-052-1

365

Days of

SLOW-COOKING

KAREN BELLESSA PETERSEN

Covenant Communications, Inc.

THE STORY BEHIND THE 365 DAYS OF MADNESS . . .

One day I decided to cook a meal in my slow-cooker. I rarely used my slow-cooker because I really had only one good recipe. The next day, I decided to try it again. I did this for about seven days as a funny little experiment. By the end of that first week I found I liked the freedom that came from having at least part of dinner completed early in the day instead of wrestling with two cranky, hungry children while cooking at 5 PM. The thought came to me, *I wonder if I could do this for a year?* I decided that at the end of the year I could compile the recipes into a cookbook.

I mentioned my 365-day experiment to my family and one of my sisters asked, "Why don't you track your progress with recipes and photos on a blog?" The blog (http://www.365daysofcrockpot.blogspot.com) was a brilliant idea, because it gave me a reason to keep working toward my goal instead of just quitting at day forty-seven (believe me, I would have). The idea took off, and here I am—having completed all 365 days!

The responses of the many moms, cooks, and blog followers amaze me. They can't wait to see what I'm cooking next and what recipe will be easy and tasty enough to add to their family's repertoire. I've loved the slow-cooking but I never realized how much work I would have to put into discovering new recipes, making adjustments to old ones, and improvising with what I had in my pantry. I'm constantly looking for recipes and ideas to pull together a menu for the next week. The biggest challenge I've faced, though, is cooking food that my family will happily eat.

I hope you enjoy the fruits of my hard work. And I hope you have fun cooking new and delicious meals for your family while you enjoy the extra time you get from using a slow-cooker!

Karen Bellessa Petersen

KAREN'S TIPS FOR SLOW-COOKING

As far as I'm concerned, slow-cooking is the only way to cook (at least most of the time). It saves time, can be very versatile (check out all the different recipes in this book!), frees up oven space, is great for busy families, works really well for serving in shifts, can save money, is energy efficient, and doesn't heat up your whole kitchen when it's hot outside. Slow-cookers are a great way to simplify your life and to give you more time to spend with those you love. Prep and cleanup are fairly easy, and your family will love the new recipes you try.

I'd love to share some tips I've found very helpful.

Buying a Slow-Cooker

- Oval slow-cookers cook more evenly and can accommodate odd-size cuts of meat.
- Buy a slow-cooker with a removable insert to make cleanup a cinch.
- If you're going to be out of the house, buy a slow-cooker with a timer that can automatically switch to warm after the cook time is up.
- Buy a slow-cooker that's fit for the size of your family. The insert crock should be at least half filled for best results. When cooking soups or stews, leave a two-inch space at the top of the crock so the dish can come to a simmer.
  - For a family of two or three, buy a two- to four-quart slow-cooker.
  - For a family of three to five, buy a five- to six-quart slow-cooker.
  - For a large family or for entertaining groups of people, opt for a seven- to eight-quart slow-cooker.
  - If you own only a very large slow-cooker and are cooking for a small group, simply place the food into an oven-safe dish that fits inside your slow-cooker. Place the dish on the bottom of the slow-cooker, cover, and cook. This will ensure that the food cooks evenly and at the right speed.
  - This cookbook does not specify which size of slow-cooker to use. Simply look at the number of servings and use the slow-cooker that matches the serving size. For example, if the recipe serves up to four people, use a two- to four-quart slow-cooker. If the recipe serves six to eight, use a larger six-quart slow-cooker.

Caring For and Cleaning a Slow-Cooker

- Fill the cooled slow-cooker insert with warm, soapy water and let soak; clean with a soft rag. Don't use an abrasive cleaner or a metal pad, because those will scratch the surface.

- To remove stains on your slow-cooker, simply fill it with water and add 1 C. of white vinegar. Cover and cook on high for two hours.

- The ceramic insert in a slow-cooker can crack if exposed to abrupt temperature shifts. Make sure the insert is cool before placing it in a cold sink. Don't put your slow-cooker on top of the stovetop or in the microwave. Read your slow-cooker manual to see if the insert is microwave-safe.

- Spray the inside of the slow-cooker with nonstick cooking spray to make cleanup easier. Or, for easier cleanup, use slow-cooker liners.

How a Slow-Cooker Works

- The slow-cooker uses indirect heat and doesn't scorch! You don't need to stir unless the recipe specifically instructs you to.

- Don't lift the lid (especially for the first two hours). Every time the lid is lifted the built-up steam escapes, and you must add twenty to thirty minutes to the cook time.

- The slow-cooker uses moist heat to cook the food and is best for less tender cuts of meat. Look for cuts of meat with lots of connective tissue. The simmering and steam converts the collagen to gelatin and the food becomes fork-tender.

- There's no need to buy more expensive cuts of meat, so look for inexpensive cuts. Some great cuts of meat for the slow-cooker include:

    Chicken on the bone or boneless, skinless chicken thighs (chicken should cook only on low for a total of four to six hours). If you end up using boneless, skinless breasts (which I don't recommend), limit the cook time to three or four hours. Chicken breasts don't have enough collagen or fat and they dry out quickly.

    For beef, look on the label for the words "pot roast" or "simmering." The best cuts are from the chuck or shoulder: boneless beef chuck roast, top or bottom blade pot roast, and cross-rib pot roast. You can also use brisket, short rib, or lean ground beef. Many recipes call for stew meat, and I prefer to make my own. Not only does it save money, but you ensure that the meat is all from the same cut so it cooks evenly. My favorite is using a chuck roast and cutting it into one-inch cubes.

    If you're using pork, look for country-style ribs, picnic roast, shoulder blade (butt) roasts, or pork steaks

Get to Know Your Slow-Cooker

Every slow-cooker cooks differently! Get to know your slow-cooker and determine how to adjust the recipe cook times according to how fast/slow your slow-cooker cooks.

To test whether your slow-cooker is cooking too hot:

+ Fill your slow-cooker two-thirds full with room-temperature water.

+ Cover and cook on high or low for six hours. (Some cookers run hotter on low and some cookers run hotter on high, so you many want to test both settings.)

+ At the end of six hours, check the water temperature with a thermometer. The water should be 195–205 degrees. If it varies from that very much, you will have to adjust the recipe cook times to fit your slow-cooker.

Food Gets Runny

There is no chance for liquids to condense in the slow-cooker—condensation constantly drips onto the food and makes it more runny. There are several ways you can thicken sauces:

+ Remove the lid and cook on high for the last half hour of cooking time.

+ Mix 1 Tbsp. cornstarch with 1 Tbsp. water until smooth; stir into the sauce and cook on high without the lid for 30 minutes.

+ Add 1–2 Tbsp. quick-cooking tapioca to the sauce at the beginning of the cook time.

+ Dredge any meat in ¼ C. flour before adding it to the slow-cooker.

+ Make a roux on the stove and stir into the sauce.

+ Transfer the liquid from the slow-cooker to a saucepan and reduce it on the stovetop.

Remember, flavors become bland and muted after cooking all day. Make sure you salt and pepper to taste and add in additional spices to taste before serving!

Reducing Fat

+ Trim all visible fat from meat before adding the meat to the slow-cooker.

+ Brown meat and drain the grease before adding the meat to the slow-cooker.

+ If cooking meat with high fat content, place thick slices of onion under the meat so it will not sit in (and cook in) the fat; you can also place the meat on a small rack that fits inside your cooker.

+ Take the lid off the slow-cooker at the end of the cooking time and let the food rest for ten minutes. Spoon off any grease that rises to the top.

Foil Collar and Foil Sling

+ Most slow-cookers have a hotter side that can cause casseroles and other dense dishes, like meatloaf, to burn. To compensate, line the slow-cooker with a foil collar: Layer and fold sheets of heavy-duty foil until you have a six-layer foil rectangle. Press the collar into the "hot" side of the slow-cooker insert; the food will help hold the collar in place during cooking.

+ For recipes that you want to lift out of the insert intact—like lasagnas, breakfast casseroles, meatloaf, and some desserts—make a foil sling. Line the slow-cooker insert with a foil collar. Then fit two large sheets of foil into the slow-cooker, perpendicular to one another, with the extra hanging over the edges of the cooker insert. Before serving, these overhanging edges can be used as handles to pull the dish out fully intact.

TABLE OF CONTENTS

 Karen's personal favorites—the ones she turns to repeatedly

 Especially easy recipes that take two minutes or less to prepare

 Good recipes to use if you're going to be gone all day

APPETIZERS

Whether you're entertaining a crowd or just making dinner for two, start off the meal on a delicious note with a scrumptious appetizer or savory dip.

Snack

get together

mix

dip   savory   Appetizing

party platter

salsa

meatballs

Hummus   display

Hot bean dip

holidays

spread   cheese fondue

Artichoke

Ingredients

1 9-oz. bag frozen spinach, thawed

1 14-oz. can quartered artichoke hearts, drained

1 C. shredded Swiss cheese

½ C. Alfredo sauce

½ C. mayonnaise

¾ tsp. garlic salt

¼ tsp. pepper

Ingredients

½ C. wheat

4 C. water

1 tsp. salt

½ yellow onion, chopped

1 green bell pepper, chopped

1 bunch green onions, chopped

1 jalapeno pepper, chopped

1 Tbsp. minced garlic

2–3 fresh tomatoes, chopped

1 8-oz. bottle zesty Italian dressing

½ tsp. ground coriander

1 bunch fresh cilantro, chopped

1 14-oz. can black beans, rinsed and drained

1 14-oz. can white beans, rinsed and drained

ARTICHOKE AND SPINACH DIP

1. Drain spinach. Dry with paper towels to absorb as much liquid as possible.

2. Rinse artichoke hearts and cut coarsely.

3. Place spinach, artichoke hearts, Swiss cheese, Alfredo sauce, mayonnaise, garlic salt, and pepper in slow-cooker. Stir to combine.

4. Cover and cook on LOW for 3–4 hours or on HIGH for 1½–2 hours.

5. Serve dip with French bread slices, chips, or crackers.

Makes 16 servings.

TEXAS CAVIAR

1. Place wheat, water, and salt in slow-cooker.

2. Cover and cook on LOW for 8 hours or on HIGH for 4 hours. Drain.

3. In a large bowl, combine cooked wheat and all the remaining ingredients. Cover bowl and chill in the refrigerator for 2 hours before serving.

4. Serve as a salsa with tortilla chips.

Makes 15 servings.

ARTICHOKE CAESAR DIP

1. Spray small slow-cooker with nonstick cooking spray.

2. Place all ingredients in slow-cooker. Stir to combine.

3. Cover and cook on LOW 2–3 hours or on HIGH for 1–1 ½ hours, or until hot.

4. Stir until dip is well blended and smooth.

5. Serve with bread or crackers. (Dip can be held on low heat setting as long as 1 hour.)

Makes 16 servings.

Ingredients

1 14-oz. can quartered artichoke hearts, drained and coarsely chopped

1 8-oz. pkg. cream cheese, cut into cubes

¼ C. shredded Swiss cheese

½ C. creamy Caesar dressing

¾ C. Parmesan cheese

⅛ tsp. red pepper flakes

CHICKEN ARTICHOKE DIP

1. Drain spinach. Dry with paper towels to absorb as much liquid as possible.

2. Rinse artichoke hearts and cut coarsely.

3. Place spinach, artichoke hearts, Alfredo sauce, mayonnaise, cream cheese, chicken, garlic, lemon juice, mozzarella cheese, and Swiss cheese in slow-cooker. Stir until combined.

4. Cover and cook on LOW for 3–4 hours or on HIGH for 1½–2 hours.

5. Sprinkle with Parmesan cheese and paprika. Serve with toasted French bread slices, chips, or crackers.

Makes 24 servings.

Ingredients

1 16-oz. bag frozen spinach, thawed

2 14-oz. cans artichoke hearts, drained

1 10-oz. jar Alfredo sauce

½ C. mayonnaise

1 8-oz. pkg. cream cheese

2 C. cooked and cubed chicken

3 garlic cloves, minced

2 Tbsp. lemon juice

1 C. shredded mozzarella cheese

1 C. shredded Swiss cheese

½ C. Parmesan cheese

½ tsp. paprika

Ingredients

1 C. dried chickpeas
4 C. water
4 garlic cloves, minced
2 Tbsp. lemon juice
1 tsp. salt
2 Tbsp. water

EASY HUMMUS

1. Rinse chickpeas and place in slow-cooker with 4 C. water.

2. Cover and cook on LOW for 6 hours or on HIGH for 3 hours, until very soft.

3. Drain liquid, retaining ¼ C.

4. Using a potato masher or hand mixer, cream the chickpeas.

5. Stir the garlic, lemon juice, salt, 2 Tbsp. water, and ¼ C. liquid into creamed chickpeas and blend well.

6. Refrigerate, if desired; serve with fresh veggies or spread on pita bread.

Makes 24 servings.

Ingredients

1 bag frozen meatballs
   (about 40–50)
1 12-oz. bottle chili sauce
1 10-oz. jar grape jelly

COCKTAIL MEATBALLS

1. Place frozen meatballs in slow-cooker.

2. In a small bowl, combine chili sauce and grape jelly; pour over the meatballs.

3. Cover and cook on LOW for 4–6 hours or on HIGH for 2–3 hours.

4. Turn slow-cooker to WARM and serve directly out of the slow-cooker.

Makes 15 servings.

Ingredients

1 3-lb. bag frozen meatballs
1 12-oz. bottle chili sauce
1 10-oz. jar grape jelly
¼ C. A1 Steak Sauce®

PARTY MEATBALLS

1. Dump the bag of meatballs into the slow-cooker.

2. In a small bowl, combine the chili sauce, grape jelly, and steak sauce.

3. Pour sauce over meatballs.

4. Cover slow-cooker and cook on LOW for 4 hours or on HIGH for 2 hours.

5. Serve as an appetizer or as the entree.

Makes 10 servings.

Ingredients

1 8-oz. can tomato sauce

1½ tsp. Italian seasoning

1 tsp. oregano

1 tsp. garlic powder

SAVORY DIPPING SAUCE

1. Place all ingredients in slow-cooker and stir to combine.

2. Cover and cook on LOW for 1–2 hours.

3. Serve warm with breadsticks.

Makes 4 servings.

Ingredients

1 32-oz. box Velveeta® cheese

1 14-oz. can Rotel® tomatoes

1 lb. lean ground beef, browned and drained

VELVEETA®–ROTEL® DIP

1. Cut cheese into 1-inch cubes and place in slow-cooker.

2. Stir in tomatoes and beef.

3. Cover and cook on HIGH for about 2 hours or until cheese is melted and hot.

4. Stir until creamy.

5. Serve with tortilla chips.

Makes 24 servings.

Ingredients

1 8-oz. pkg. cream cheese

1 14-oz. can Rotel® tomatoes

CREAM CHEESE–ROTEL® DIP

1. Cut cream cheese into 1-inch cubes.

2. Place cream cheese and tomatoes in small slow-cooker.

3. Cover and cook on HIGH for 1–2 hours

4. Stir until creamy.

5. Serve as a dip for chips, crackers, or vegetables.

Makes 16 servings.

EASY CHEESY FONDUE

1. Combine all ingredients in slow-cooker and stir to combine.
2. Cover and cook on LOW for 2–3 hours or on HIGH for 1–1½ hours.
3. Stir with a whisk until creamy.
4. Serve with bread and veggies.

Makes 16 servings.

Ingredients

2 10¾-oz. cans condensed cheese soup

2 C. grated sharp cheddar cheese

1 Tbsp. Worcestershire sauce

1 tsp. lemon juice

2 Tbsp. dried chopped chives

HOT BEAN DIP

1. Combine all ingredients in slow-cooker.
2. Cover and cook on LOW for 3–4 hours or on HIGH for 1½–2 hours.
3. Stir until creamy.
4. Serve hot with tortilla chips.

Makes 16 servings.

Ingredients

1 16-oz. can refried beans

1 C. salsa

2 C. shredded Monterey Jack and cheddar cheese

1 C. sour cream

3 oz. cream cheese, cubed

1 Tbsp. chili powder

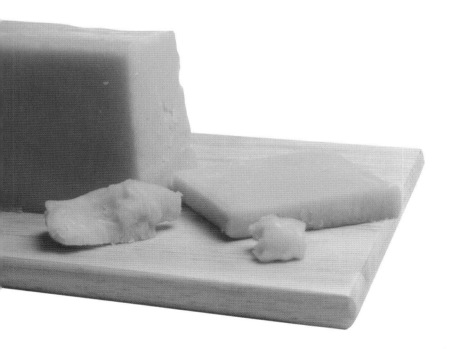

BEVERAGES

Use your bumper crop of tomatoes to make a tangy glass of tomato juice or wow your holiday guests with the aroma of your spiced wassail—either way, your slow-cooker is your third hand.

tomato juice

hot

sweet

punch Cider

Christmas cranberry punch

Refreshing holidays

chocolate

cool spice wassail

mix

Ingredients

10–12 fresh, large tomatoes

½ tsp. salt

1 tsp. seasoned salt

¼ tsp. pepper

1 Tbsp. sugar

FRESH TOMATO JUICE

1. Wash and drain tomatoes.

2. Remove cores and blossom ends and place tomatoes in slow-cooker.

3. Cover and cook on LOW for 4–6 hours or on HIGH for 2–3 hours, or until tomatoes are soft.

4. Place tomatoes in blender and liquefy.

5. Stir in salt, seasoned salt, pepper, and sugar.

6. Chill and serve.

Makes 6 servings.

HOLIDAY HOT COCOA

1. In slow-cooker, combine powdered milk, cocoa, sugar, and salt.

2. Use a whisk to stir ingredients until there are no lumps.

3. Pour in hot water and stir.

4. Cover and cook on LOW for 2 hours or on HIGH for 1 hour.

5. Turn to warm and serve.

Makes 7 servings.

Ingredients

1 C. nonfat dried powdered milk

5 Tbsp. cocoa powder

5 Tbsp. sugar

¼ tsp. salt

5 C. hot water

SPICED WASSAIL

1. Place cloves, cinnamon sticks, and allspice in a piece of cheesecloth; tie shut with kitchen string. Place in large slow-cooker.

2. Add orange juice, water, apple cider, lemonade, and sugar to the slow-cooker.

3. Cover and cook on LOW for 6–8 hours.

4. Turn to warm and serve in mugs.

Makes 15 servings.

Ingredients

12 whole cloves

4 cinnamon sticks

2 tsp. allspice

1 6-oz. can frozen orange juice

6½ C. water

½ gal. apple cider

1 6-oz. can frozen lemonade

½ C. sugar

CHRISTMAS CRANBERRY PUNCH

1. In slow-cooker, combine all ingredients and stir until sugar is dissolved.

2. Cover and cook on LOW for 3–5 hours.

3. Turn to warm and serve in mugs.

Makes 7 servings.

Ingredients

4 C. hot water

6 Tbsp. sugar

2 C. cranberry juice

½ C. orange juice

2 Tbsp. lemon juice

¼ tsp. ground cloves

1 cinnamon stick

¼ C. red hot candies

BREADS/SPREADS

Slow-cooker bread is a wonderful way to bake in the summertime when you don't want to heat up the house with your oven. You also don't have to worry about getting home to take the bread out of the oven!

baked

spread

loaf **butter**

savory

peanut butter

moist

toast

zucchini

Cheese slice

banana yeast muffin

whole-wheat

bread

Ingredients

1 C. fat-free cottage cheese

4 egg whites

1 C. sugar

¾ C. fat-free milk

1 tsp. vanilla

2¾ C. Bisquick® baking mix

½ C. dried cranberries

2 Tbsp. orange zest

COTTAGE CHEESE BREAD

1. In a medium bowl, mix all ingredients.

2. Pour batter into greased slow-cooker.

3. Cover and cook on HIGH for 2 hours.

Makes 8 servings.

Ingredients

2 C. warm, reconstituted powdered milk

1 Tbsp. white vinegar

2 Tbsp. canola oil

¼ C. brown sugar

¾ tsp. salt

2¼ tsp. yeast

2½ C. whole-wheat flour

1¼ C. white flour

HEALTHY WHOLE-WHEAT BREAD

1. In a large bowl, combine milk, vinegar, oil, brown sugar, salt, yeast, half the whole-wheat flour, and half the white flour. Beat with mixer for 2 minutes.

2. Add remaining flour and mix well.

3. Place dough in well-greased bread or cake pan that fits in slow-cooker. Cover pan loosely with greased aluminum foil and let stand for 5 minutes.

4. Place a wire rack or balls of crumpled foil in the bottom of the slow-cooker and place pan on top.

5. Place a thick paper towel over the top of the slow-cooker and place the lid on top of the paper towel to seal the slow-cooker.

6. Cover slow-cooker and cook on HIGH for 2–3 hours. Remove pan and let stand for 5 minutes. Serve warm.

Makes 1 loaf (8 servings).

WHOLE-WHEAT BANANA BREAD

1. Spray a large slow-cooker with nonstick cooking spray and dust with flour.

2. In large bowl, cream butter with electric mixer until fluffy. Slowly add sugar, eggs, and mashed bananas. Beat until smooth. Set aside.

3. In small bowl, sift together flour, baking powder, salt, and baking soda. Slowly beat flour mixture into creamed mixture.

4. Pour batter into the slow-cooker.

5. Place a thick paper towel across the top of the slow-cooker and place the lid on top of the paper towel to seal the slow-cooker.

6. Cook on HIGH for 2–3 hours or until toothpick inserted near center of bread comes out clean.

7. Let cool, then turn bread out of slow-cooker onto plate or serving platter.

Makes 1 loaf (8 servings).

Ingredients

⅓ C. unsalted butter, softened

⅔ C. sugar

2 eggs

3 medium ripe bananas, mashed

1¾ C. whole-wheat flour

2 tsp. baking powder

¼ tsp. salt

¼ tsp. baking soda

Ingredients

2½ C. flour

½ C. sugar

½ C. brown sugar

3½ tsp. baking powder

1 tsp. salt

3 Tbsp. canola oil

⅓ C. milk

1 egg

2–3 medium ripe bananas, mashed

LOW-FAT BANANA BREAD

1. In a large bowl, combine all ingredients; beat for 30 seconds.

2. Pour batter into a greased bread pan that is small enough to fit inside your slow-cooker.

3. Place a small rack on the bottom of the slow-cooker; if you don't have a rack, use crumpled balls of aluminum foil.

4. Place the bread pan on top of the rack or foil so that air can circulate around the bread pan.

5. Place a thick paper towel across the top of the slow-cooker and place the lid on top of the paper towel to seal the slow-cooker.

6. Cook on HIGH for 2–3 hours or until toothpick inserted near center of bread comes out clean.

7. Remove bread pan from slow-cooker, let cool, and serve.

Makes 1 loaf (8 servings).

Ingredients

4 lbs. cooking apples

2 C. apple cider

3 C. sugar

2 tsp. cinnamon

⅛ tsp. allspice

1 tsp. ground cloves, optional

APPLE BUTTER

1. Stem, core, and quarter apples (do not peel).

2. In a large slow-cooker, combine apples and cider; cover.

3. Cook on LOW for 8–10 hours.

4. Stir in sugar and spices and continue cooking for 1 more hour.

5. Remove from heat and cool thoroughly.

6. Use a blender or food processor to blend in the skins.

7. Freeze in pint-sized containers or pour into hot sterilized jars and seal.

Makes 4–5 pints apple butter.

Ingredients

1 egg

¼ C. sugar

¼ C. brown sugar

¼ C. canola oil

½ oz. unsweetened chocolate

½ C. grated zucchini

¼ tsp. vanilla

½ C. flour

¼ tsp. salt

¼ tsp. cinnamon

⅛ tsp. allspice

⅛ tsp. baking powder

¼ tsp. baking soda

CHOCOLATE ZUCCHINI BREAD

1. In a large mixing bowl, beat the eggs until they are lemon-colored and smooth. Beat in the sugar, brown sugar, and oil. Add the chocolate. Stir in zucchini and vanilla.

2. Sift all dry ingredients; stir into the zucchini mixture.

3. Pour into well-greased loaf pan that will fit inside a large slow-cooker.

4. Place a wire rack or balls of crumpled foil in the bottom of the slow-cooker and place pan on top of rack.

5. Place a thick paper towel across the top of the slow-cooker and place the lid on top of the paper towel to seal the slow-cooker.

6. Cook on HIGH for 2–3 hours or until toothpick inserted near center of bread comes out clean.

7. Remove bread pan from slow-cooker, let cool, and serve.

Makes 1 loaf (8 servings).

BROWN SUGAR BANANA BREAD

1. In a medium bowl, combine flour, baking powder, baking soda, and salt. Mix well. Set aside.

2. In a large bowl, beat butter with sugar and brown sugar until creamed. Blend in egg, milk, bananas, and vanilla.

3. Add dry mixture to wet mixture; beat for 30 seconds.

4. Pour batter into greased bread pan that fits inside slow-cooker.

5. Place a wire rack or balls of crumpled foil in bottom of large slow-cooker. Place pan in slow-cooker.

6. Place a thick paper towel across the top of the slow-cooker and place the lid on top of the paper towel to seal the slow-cooker.

7. Cook on HIGH for 2–3 hours or until toothpick inserted near center of bread comes out clean.

8. Remove bread pan from slow-cooker, let cool, and serve.

Makes 1 loaf (8 servings).

Ingredients

1¾ C. flour

1 tsp. baking powder

½ tsp. baking soda

¼ tsp. salt

¼ C. butter, softened

¼ C. sugar

½ C. brown sugar

1 egg

⅓ C. skim milk

3 medium ripe bananas, mashed

1 tsp. vanilla

BREAKFAST

Breakfast can be a cinch to prepare and keep warm in your slow-cooker. It's perfect for busy mornings, serving in shifts, or even hosting a brunch!

apple oatmeal
waffle eggs
granola
casserole
French toast
morning
banana Sunshine
sausage start

Ingredients

⅓ C. oil

½ C. sugar

1 large egg, beaten

2 C. dry quick oats

1½ tsp. baking powder

½ tsp. salt

¾ C. milk

Ingredients

4 C. water

1½ C. apple juice

1 C. steel-cut oats

½ C. pearl barley (regular, not quick-cooking)

1 tsp. ground cinnamon

½ tsp. grated fresh ginger

¼ tsp. salt

Optional Toppings:
Toasted pecans
Chopped apple
Brown sugar
Honey

BAKED OATMEAL

1. Pour oil into slow-cooker to grease bottom and sides.

2. Add remaining ingredients to slow-cooker and mix well.

3. Cover and bake on LOW for 2½–3 hours.

Serves 4–6.

APPLE-CINNAMON OATMEAL

1. In a slow-cooker, combine water, apple juice, oats, barley, cinnamon, ginger, and salt.

2. Cover and cook on LOW for 5–7 hours.

3. Top with your preferred toppings and serve.

Makes 8 servings.

CRANBERRY-RAISIN STEEL-CUT OATS

1. Spray slow-cooker with nonstick cooking spray.
2. In a small (1½- to 3-quart) slow-cooker, combine all ingredients.
3. Cover and cook on LOW for 5–7 hours.
4. Serve with milk or cream, if desired.

Makes 4 servings.

Ingredients

1 C. steel-cut oats
½ C. dried cranberries
½ C. raisins
3½ C. water
½ tsp. salt

BREAKFAST HASH

1. Put all ingredients in a greased slow-cooker and stir to combine.
2. Cover and cook on LOW for 3–4 hours.
3. Serve with grated cheese and salsa.

Makes 6 servings.

Ingredients

1 lb. bulk breakfast sausage, browned and drained
2 C. diced and peeled potatoes
2 Tbsp. chopped onion
6 eggs, beaten
2 Tbsp. milk

BREAKFAST CASSEROLE

1. In a greased slow-cooker, combine eggs, sausage, milk, cheddar, bread, salt, and mustard.
2. Sprinkle mozzarella over the top.
3. Cover and cook for 2 hours on HIGH, then for 1 hour on LOW.

Makes 6 servings.

Ingredients

6 eggs, beaten
1½ lbs. bulk breakfast sausage, browned and drained
1½ C. milk
1 C. shredded cheddar cheese
8 slices bread, torn into pieces
1 tsp. salt
½ tsp. dry mustard
1 C. shredded mozzarella

Ingredients

4 large eggs

½ C. milk

1 tsp. cinnamon

6 slices stale or toasted French bread, cubed

Maple syrup

FRENCH TOAST CASSEROLE

1. Spray slow-cooker with nonstick cooking spray.

2. In a small bowl, mix the eggs, milk, and cinnamon with a whisk.

3. Place 2 slices of cubed bread in bottom of slow-cooker. Pour ½ C. egg mixture over the bread.

4. Add 2 more slices of bread. Pour another ½ C. egg mixture over the bread.

5. Add the final cubes of bread and the final egg mixture.

6. Push down the bread so that all of it is moistened.

7. Cover and cook on HIGH for 2 hours.

8. Spoon onto a plate, drizzle with maple syrup, and serve.

Makes 6 servings.

Ingredients

4 eggs

4 C. boiling water

POACHED EGGS

1. Pour boiling water into the bottom of a large slow-cooker.

2. Cover and heat on HIGH for 20 minutes.

3. Spray 4 custard cups with nonstick cooking spray. Break one egg into each cup.

4. Place the custard cups into the slow-cooker in a single layer; cover and cook on HIGH for 12 minutes.

5. Test eggs for doneness. Eggs are done when the white is solid but the yolk is soft. If the egg white is still runny, cover the slow-cooker and cook a few minutes longer until the whites are set.

Makes 4 servings.

Ingredients

1 24-oz. carton small-curd cottage cheese

1 10-oz. bag frozen chopped broccoli, thawed and drained

2 C. shredded cheddar cheese

6 eggs, beaten

⅓ C. flour

¼ C. melted butter

½ tsp. salt

Shredded cheese (optional)

EGG AND BROCCOLI CASSEROLE

1. In a greased slow-cooker, combine cottage cheese, broccoli, cheddar cheese, eggs, flour, butter, and salt.

2. Cover and cook on HIGH for 1 hour.

3. Stir and reduce heat to LOW.

4. Cover and cook on LOW for 2–4 hours or until eggs are set.

5. Sprinkle with cheese and serve.

Makes 6 servings.

Ingredients

½ lb. bulk breakfast sausage, browned and drained

4 waffles, toasted and cubed

1 C. shredded cheddar cheese

¾ C. evaporated milk

4 oz. cream cheese

3 eggs

½ tsp. dry mustard

Maple syrup

WAFFLE AND SAUSAGE BREAKFAST

1. In a slow-cooker, layer sausage, waffle cubes, and cheese.

2. In a skillet, heat milk and cream cheese over low heat until cheese melts and mixture is smooth.

3. Remove skillet from heat; beat in the eggs, one at a time, until smooth. Stir in the dry mustard.

4. Pour contents of skillet into the slow-cooker.

5. Cover and cook on LOW for about 4–5 hours or until eggs are set.

6. Serve with warmed maple syrup.

Makes 4–5 servings.

CARAMEL ROLLS

1. In a small bowl, mix sugar and cinnamon. Set aside.

2. Dip individual biscuits into melted butter and then into cinnamon-sugar mixture.

3. Place each covered biscuit in greased 3½- to 5-quart slow-cooker.

4. Cover and cook on HIGH for 2½–3 hours, or until rolls are done. You can check the rolls in the center for doneness after 2 hours.

Makes 6–8 servings.

Ingredients

½ C. brown sugar

½ tsp. cinnamon

2 8-oz. pkg. refrigerator biscuits

¼ C. melted butter

PEANUT BUTTER GRANOLA

1. In a large slow-cooker, combine oats, wheat germ, coconut, sunflower seeds, and raisins.

2. In a small saucepan, melt the butter, peanut butter, and brown sugar over low heat.

3. Pour the peanut butter mixture over the oat mixture in the slow-cooker; mix well.

4. Cover and cook on LOW for 1½ hours, stirring every 15 minutes.

5. Allow to cool on cookie sheet; break into chunks when cooled. Store in airtight container.

Makes 16–20 servings.

Ingredients

6 C. quick oats

½ C. wheat germ

½ C. toasted coconut

½ C. sunflower seeds

½ C. raisins

1 C. butter

1 C. peanut butter

1 C. brown sugar

BEEF DISHES

Beef: It's what's for dinner! That's never more true than when you're using your slow-cooker to prepare a delicious and comforting meal for your family.

Meat
Ribs medium
dinner Beef casserole
Roast Gyros
stroganoff
French dip
beef curry
Burritos sloppy Joes
shredded
pot roast
sandwich
Delicious chow mein Steak

Ingredients

¾ lb. extra-lean ground beef

¾ lb. bulk Italian sausage

¼ C. chopped onion

2 garlic cloves, minced

2 tsp. Italian seasoning

¼ C. dry bread crumbs

1 egg, slightly beaten

1 28-oz. jar marinara sauce

Ingredients

¾ lb. extra-lean ground beef or ground turkey

1 C. skim milk

½ C. instant brown rice

¼ C. chopped onion

1 C. dry bread crumbs

½ tsp. salt

Dash of black pepper

1 10¾-oz. can low-fat, low-sodium cream of mushroom soup

½ C. skim milk

ITALIAN MEATBALLS

1. In a medium bowl, mix beef, sausage, onion, garlic, Italian seasoning, bread crumbs, and egg.

2. Shape mixture into 24 1½- inch balls.

3. Place a wire rack in the bottom of the slow-cooker; place meatballs on rack.

4. Cover and cook on HIGH for 2–3 hours.

5. Serve meatballs with spaghetti, if desired; pour warmed marinara sauce over the top.

Makes 6 servings.

LOW-FAT PORCUPINE MEATBALLS

1. In a medium bowl, combine meat, 1 C. skim milk, rice, onion, bread crumbs, salt, and pepper.

2. Shape mixture into meatballs.

3. Place in the bottom of a slow-cooker.

4. In small bowl, mix soup and ½ C. milk. Pour over the top of the meatballs.

5. Cover and cook on LOW for 4–5 hours.

6. Serve; mushroom soup mixture acts as gravy.

Makes 5 servings.

MEATBALLS AND RICE

1. In a medium bowl, combine beef, oats, egg, ¼ C. spaghetti sauce, onion, chili powder, garlic powder, and salt. Shape into meatballs.

2. Arrange meatballs in the bottom of slow-cooker.

3. Cover and cook on LOW for 4–6 hours.

4. Drain as much grease as possible from the meatballs; cover with the remaining spaghetti sauce.

5. Cover and cook for 30 additional minutes.

6. Sprinkle mozzarella cheese over the meatballs and serve over hot, cooked rice.

Makes 4 servings.

Ingredients

1 lb. ground beef

½ C. quick oats

1 egg

1 28-oz. can spaghetti sauce, divided

¼ C. chopped onion

1 tsp. chili powder

½ tsp. garlic powder

½ tsp. salt

1 egg

Shredded mozzarella cheese

Hot, cooked rice

Ingredients

1 egg

¼ C. milk

2 slices bread, cubed

¼ C. chopped onions

2 Tbsp. chopped green peppers

1 tsp. salt

¼ tsp. pepper

1½ lbs. extra-lean ground beef

¼ C. ketchup

8 small red potatoes

4–6 medium carrots, cut into 1-inch chunks

MEATLOAF DINNER

1. In a large bowl, beat egg and milk. Stir in bread cubes, onions, green peppers, salt, and pepper. Add beef and mix well.

2. Shape into a loaf that is about an inch smaller in circumference than the inside of the slow-cooker.

3. Place loaf into slow-cooker. Spread top with ketchup.

4. Place carrots and potatoes around meatloaf.

5. Cover and cook on HIGH for 1 hour. Reduce heat and cook on LOW for 5–6 additional hours.

Makes 5 servings.

BARBECUE MEATBALLS

1. In a small bowl, mix barbecue sauce, orange juice, cranberry sauce, ground mustard, ginger, and salt.

2. Place meatballs in slow-cooker and pour sauce over the top, coating the meatballs as much as possible.

3. Cover and cook on LOW for 2 hours.

4. Turn to WARM and serve out of slow-cooker.

Makes 6 servings.

Ingredients

1 C. barbecue sauce

¾ C. orange juice

1 16-oz. can jellied cranberry sauce

½ tsp. ground mustard

½ tsp. ground ginger

½ tsp. salt

2 lbs. frozen meatballs

BEEF AND POTATO CASSEROLE

1. Spray large nonstick skillet with cooking spray. Put ground beef in skillet; sprinkle with onion powder and garlic powder. Cook over medium heat, stirring frequently, until beef is browned and crumbled. Drain well.

2. In a medium bowl, combine onions, soup, and pepper; mix well.

3. Arrange potato slices in bottom of slow-cooker; top with meat mixture. Pour soup mixture over top and mix.

4. Cover and cook on LOW for 4–6 hours.

5. Increase heat to HIGH. Pour half-and-half into slow-cooker. Cover and cook for 15–20 minutes; serve.

Makes 6 servings.

Ingredients

2 lbs. lean ground beef

1 tsp. onion powder

¾ tsp. garlic powder

¼ C. frozen chopped onions (thawed and drained)

1 10¾-oz. can low-fat tomato soup

½ tsp. pepper

5 medium potatoes, peeled and sliced

1 C. nonfat half-and-half

Ingredients

1 lb. extra-lean ground beef

1 small onion, chopped

1 tsp. garlic salt

¼ tsp. garlic powder

1 tsp. Worcestershire sauce

¼ C. flour

1¼ C. hot water

2 tsp. beef bouillon granules

1 6-oz. pkg. shell macaroni

1 4-oz. can mushrooms, drained

1 C. sour cream

BEEF AND PASTA CASSEROLE

1. In a medium skillet, brown the ground beef and onion; drain grease and place beef in slow-cooker.

2. Stir in the garlic salt, garlic powder, Worcestershire sauce, and flour. Add water and bouillon; mix well.

3. Cover and cook on LOW for 2–3 hours.

4. Cook macaroni per package directions.

5. Add cooked pasta, mushrooms, and sour cream to slow-cooker; stir to mix.

6. Cover and cook on HIGH for 10–15 additional minutes.

Makes 4–5 servings.

Ingredients

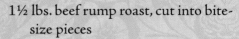

1½ lbs. beef rump roast, cut into bite-size pieces

1½ Tbsp. Shirley J® Dutch Oven and Slow-cooker Beef Seasoning

2 Tbsp. water

½ C. Shirley J® Whisk Bliss

2 C. water

½ C. sour cream

1 C. fresh mushrooms

BEEF ROAST STROGANOFF

1. In slow-cooker, place pieces of roast. Sprinkle beef seasoning over meat and stir to coat. Pour 2 Tbsp. water over the meat and stir, getting each piece of meat coated with seasoning.

2. In a saucepan, combine Whisk Bliss and 2 C. water. Whisk and bring to a slow boil. Pour into the slow-cooker.

3. Cover and cook on LOW for 6–8 hours, or until meat is very tender.

4. Add sour cream and mushrooms. Cover and cook for another 10–15 minutes. Serve over rice or noodles.

Makes 4–6 servings.

Ingredients

2 lbs. beef stew meat

1 large onion, chopped

1 10¾-oz. can cream of golden mushroom soup

1 10¾-oz. can cream of onion soup

2 4-oz. cans sliced mushrooms, drained

¼ tsp. pepper

1 8-oz. pkg. cream cheese

1 C. sour cream

6 C. hot noodles or rice

GOLDEN BEEF STROGANOFF

1. In slow-cooker, mix beef, onion, soups, mushrooms, and pepper.

2. Cover and cook on LOW for 6–8 hours or until beef is very tender.

3. Stir cream cheese and sour cream into beef mixture until melted.

4. Serve beef and sauce over noodles or rice.

Makes 8 servings.

BEEF STROGANOFF WITH RICE

1. In slow-cooker, mix stew meat and dry soup mix until evenly coated. Top with mushrooms and soup.

2. Cover and cook on LOW for 6–8 hours.

3. Just before serving, stir sour cream and cream cheese into beef mixture until smooth.

4. Serve over hot, cooked rice.

Makes 5 servings.

Ingredients

1½ lbs. beef stew meat

2 Tbsp. onion soup mix

1 4-oz. can mushrooms, drained

1 10¾-oz. can cream of mushroom soup

½ C. sour cream

4 oz. cream cheese

SPRITE® STROGANOFF

1. In slow-cooker, combine roast, Sprite®, onion soup mix, and cream of mushroom soup.

2. Cover and cook on LOW for 6–8 hours.

3. Stir in mushrooms and sour cream. Warm for an additional 15 minutes; serve over rice or noodles.

Makes 4 servings.

Ingredients

1½ lbs. pot roast, cut into cubes, or 1½ lbs. stew meat

¼ C. Sprite®

½ pkg. onion soup mix (.5 oz.)

1 10¾-oz. can cream of mushroom soup

½ C. sour cream

1 C. sliced mushrooms

Hot rice or noodles

Ingredients

2 lbs. beef stew meat

Salt and pepper

½ small onion, chopped

1 4-oz. can mushrooms, drained

1 10¾-oz. can cream of chicken soup

1 8-oz. can tomato sauce

2 tsp. dried parsley

1 C. sour cream

STEW MEAT STROGANOFF

1. In slow-cooker, combine stew meat, salt and pepper, onion, mushrooms, and soup.

2. Cover and cook on LOW for 6–7 hours (until stew meat is tender).

3. Add tomato sauce, parsley, and sour cream; cover and cook until heated through.

4. Serve over noodles or rice.

Makes 6 servings.

Ingredients

1 lb. beef stew meat

½ pkg. dry ranch dressing mix (.5 oz.)

1 10¾-oz. can cream of mushroom soup

1 4-oz. can mushrooms, drained

½ C. sour cream

Hot rice or noodles

BEEF AND MUSHROOMS

1. In slow-cooker, arrange stew meat; sprinkle with ranch dressing mix.

2. Pour cream of mushroom soup over the top of meat.

3. Cover and cook on LOW for 6–8 hours.

4. Stir in mushrooms and sour cream.

5. Cover and cook until heated through.

6. Serve over rice or noodles.

Makes 4 servings.

SHIRLEY J® BEEF STROGANOFF

1. In a microwave-safe bowl, combine 3 tsp. Shirley J® Slow-cooker Beef Seasoning, tomato paste, onion, garlic, and oil. Microwave 4–5 minutes, stirring every minute, until onions are soft. Transfer to slow-cooker.

2. Add beef, vinegar, beef bouillon mixture, and tapioca. Stir to combine.

3. Cover and cook on LOW for 6–8 hours, until beef is very tender.

4. Add basil, 1 tsp. Shirley J® Slow-cooker Beef Seasoning, sour cream, and mushrooms. Add salt and pepper to taste.

5. Cover and cook for an additional 30 minutes; serve over noodles or rice.

Makes 4 servings.

Ingredients

4 tsp. Shirley J® Slow-cooker Beef Seasoning, divided

1 Tbsp. tomato paste

½ medium onion, finely diced

3 garlic cloves, minced

1 tsp. canola oil

1 lb. beef stew meat

1 Tbsp. white wine vinegar

½ tsp. Shirley J® beef bouillon mixed with 1 C. hot water

1 Tbsp. quick-cooking tapioca

Basil to taste

⅓ C. sour cream

1 C. fresh button mushrooms, sliced

Salt and pepper

Hot noodles or rice

Ingredients

ALL
DAY

1-lb. boneless beef chuck roast, sliced
    into thin strips

1 C. beef consommé

½ C. soy sauce

⅓ C. brown sugar

2 Tbsp. sesame oil

3 garlic cloves, minced

2 Tbsp. cornstarch

2 Tbsp. water

Fresh broccoli florets (as many as
    desired)

Hot, cooked rice

Ingredients

1½-lb. boneless beef chuck roast,
    sliced into thin strips

1 ⅓ C. beef broth

½ C. oyster sauce

½- to 1-lb. fresh broccoli florets

¼ C. water

2 Tbsp. cornstarch

Hot, cooked rice (optional)

Toasted sesame seeds (for garnish)

BEEF AND BROCCOLI

1. Place beef in slow-cooker.

2. In a small bowl, combine consommé, soy sauce, brown sugar, oil, and garlic. Pour over beef.

3. Cover and cook on LOW for 6–8 hours.

4. In a cup, stir cornstarch and water until smooth. Add to slow-cooker. Stir well to combine.

5. Blanch broccoli florets and add to the slow-cooker. Stir to combine.

6. Cover and cook for an additional 20 minutes on HIGH or until thickened. Serve over hot, cooked rice.

Makes 4–6 servings.

SESAME BEEF

1. In slow-cooker, arrange beef strips; pour beef broth and oyster sauce over the beef.

2. Cover and cook on LOW for 6–8 hours or on HIGH for 3–4 hours or until beef is very tender.

3. Place broccoli in microwave-safe bowl with ¼ C. water. Microwave 4–5 minutes, until broccoli is tender.

4. In a cup, combine cornstarch and 2 Tbsp. cooking liquid; stir until smooth. Add to slow-cooker and stir well to combine.

5. Drain the broccoli and stir into the slow-cooker.

6. Cook uncovered on HIGH for about 15 minutes or until sauce is thickened.

7. Serve over hot, cooked rice and garnish with sesame seeds.

Makes 6 servings.

Ingredients

1 lb. lean ground beef

1 medium onion, chopped

1 C. chopped celery

1 10¾-oz. can cream of chicken soup

1 10¾-oz. can cream of mushroom soup

¼ C. soy sauce

¼ can water

¾ C. cooked rice

Chow mein noodles

CHOW MEIN CASSEROLE

1. Brown beef, onion, and celery in a skillet.

2. Mix in the chicken soup, mushroom soup, soy sauce, water, and cooked rice.

3. Pour into slow-cooker and cook on LOW for 3–4 hours.

4. Sprinkle with chow mein noodles when serving.

Makes 6 servings.

Ingredients

2 Tbsp. sesame oil

2 garlic cloves, minced

1-lb. beef chuck roast, cut into bite-size pieces

2 large potatoes, peeled and cubed

3 Tbsp. Thai red curry paste

1 tsp. sugar

2 tsp. onion powder

1 14-oz. can coconut milk

Salt and pepper to taste

Hot, cooked rice

Diced tomatoes

Peanuts

ALL DAY

THAI BEEF CURRY

1. In a frying pan, heat oil; add garlic and roast. Stir and turn for about 3 minutes until meat is browned. Transfer to slow-cooker and add the potatoes.

2. In the frying pan, blend the curry paste, sugar, onion powder, and coconut milk. Season with salt and pepper. Bring to a boil; pour over the meat.

3. Cover and cook on LOW for 6–8 hours, or until meat is fork-tender.

4. Serve over hot, cooked rice and top with diced tomatoes and peanuts.

Makes 4 servings.

THAI BEEF CURRY AND CAULIFLOWER

1. In a large saucepan, heat sesame oil. Add onion, garlic, and stew meat; cook, stirring and turning, for about 3 minutes, until meat is browned.

2. Place contents of saucepan in the slow-cooker; add the potatoes.

3. In the saucepan, blend the curry paste, sugar, and coconut milk; season to taste with salt and pepper. Bring to a boil, then pour over meat.

4. Cover the slow-cooker and cook on HIGH for 3–5 hours or on LOW for 7–9 hours.

5. Blanch the cauliflower florets and add to the slow-cooker with the tomatoes and peanuts. Cover and cook on HIGH for another 30 minutes.

6. Serve over hot, cooked rice and garnish with cilantro leaves and lemon slices.

Makes 12–14 servings.

ALL DAY

Ingredients

2 Tbsp. sesame oil

1 C. chopped onion

2 garlic cloves, minced

1½ lbs. beef stew meat

2 large potatoes, peeled and cut into cubes

3 Tbsp. Thai red curry paste, mild

1 tsp. sugar

1 14-oz. can coconut milk

Salt and pepper

½ head small cauliflower, cut into small florets

½ C. peanuts

1 14-oz. can diced tomatoes, drained

Hot, cooked rice

Cilantro leaves and lemon slices for garnish

Ingredients

3-lb. boneless beef chuck roast

⅓ C. flour

2 Tbsp. curry powder

1 tsp. salt

½ tsp. pepper

1 Tbsp. canola oil

3 onions, chopped

6 garlic cloves, minced

3 green bell peppers, chopped

3 Tbsp. fresh gingerroot, minced

1 28-oz. can diced tomatoes

1 6-oz. can tomato paste

1 C. beef broth

3 Tbsp. balsamic vinegar

Hot, cooked rice

BEEF CURRY

1. Trim excess fat from beef; cut beef into 2-inch cubes.

2. On shallow plate, combine flour, curry powder, salt, and pepper. Dredge meat in flour mixture.

3. In a medium skillet, heat oil; brown the meat over medium heat for about 2 minutes on each side.

4. Place meat and drippings from skillet into the slow-cooker.

3. Add onions, garlic, bell peppers, gingerroot, tomatoes, tomato paste, and beef broth to slow-cooker.

4. Cover and cook on LOW for 6–8 hours or until beef is tender.

5. Stir in balsamic vinegar and serve over hot, cooked rice.

Makes 12–14 servings.

CAFÉ RIO SHREDDED BEEF SALAD

1. Cut the onion into large, chunky slices; place on the bottom of slow-cooker.

2. Place the roast on top of the onions.

3. Combine broth, cumin, garlic, and tomato sauce; pour over the top of the roast.

4. Cover and cook on LOW for 6–8 hours.

5. Move meat to a cutting board; use two forks to shred the beef.

6. Strain the juices from the slow-cooker, reserving the juice. Move meat back to the slow-cooker and pour strained juices over the shredded beef.

6. Stir in enchilada sauce and tomato paste.

7. Season with kosher salt and cumin to taste.

8. Serve over salad with tomatillo dressing, cilantro, lime juice, and avocado slices.

Makes 8 servings.

TOMATILLO DRESSING

1. Put all ingredients in a blender.

2. Blend until smooth and creamy.

3. Refrigerate until ready to use.

Makes 30 servings.

Ingredients

1 small onion

2-lb. boneless beef chuck roast

1 C. beef broth

1 Tbsp. ground cumin

3–5 garlic cloves, minced

1 8-oz. can tomato sauce

1 14-oz. can green enchilada sauce

1–2 Tbsp. tomato paste

Kosher salt to taste

Cumin to taste

Tomatillo dressing to taste (see recipe below left)

Cilantro, fresh lime juice, and avocado to taste

Ingredients

1 1-oz. pkg. Hidden Valley® Buttermilk Ranch mix

1 C. buttermilk

1 C. mayonnaise

2 medium tomatillos, husks removed and rinsed well

1 garlic clove, minced

1 small bunch cilantro

½ tsp. lime juice

1 small jalapeño, seeds removed

SOUTHWEST BEEF BURRITOS

1. Place roast and water in slow-cooker.

2. Cover and cook on LOW for 8–9 hours.

3. Remove meat to a cutting board; use two forks to shred the beef.

4. Skim fat from cooking liquid, setting aside ½ C. of liquid.

5. In a large skillet, cook tomatoes, green pepper, onion, garlic, and bay leaf in canola oil for 18–22 minutes, or until liquid is reduced to 2 Tbsp.

6. Stir in ketchup, jalapeño slices and juice, vinegar, salt, garlic salt, and reserved cooking liquid. Bring to a boil.

7. Stir in shredded beef; discard bay leaf and heat through.

8. Serve on soft tortilla shells.

Makes 8 servings.

Ingredients

2 lb. boneless beef chuck roast

½ C. water

4 large tomatoes, peeled and chopped

1 large green pepper, thinly sliced

1 medium onion, chopped

2 garlic cloves, minced

1 bay leaf

2 Tbsp. canola oil

¾ C. ketchup

½ C. pickled jalapeño slices

1 Tbsp. juice from jalapeño slices

1 Tbsp. vinegar

1 tsp. salt

⅛ tsp. garlic salt

Tortillas

EASY PEASY BEEF BURRITOS

1. Place roast in slow-cooker; pour the enchilada sauce over the roast.

2. Cover and cook on LOW for 6–8 hours or until beef begins to fall apart.

3. Remove roast to a cutting board; use two forks to shred the beef.

4. Serve in tortillas with desired toppings.

Makes 6–8 servings.

Ingredients

2- to 3-lb. boneless beef chuck roast

1 28-oz. can green enchilada sauce

6–8 8-inch flour tortillas

Toppings: lettuce, cilantro, tomato, cheese, and sour cream

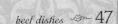

Ingredients

1-lb. flank steak

1 1.25-oz. env. taco seasoning

½ medium onion, chopped

1 4-oz. can chopped green chilies

½ Tbsp. vinegar

4–6 flour tortillas

⅔ C. shredded cheddar cheese

¾ C. diced tomatoes

½ C. sour cream

FLANK STEAK BURRITOS

1. Cut steak in half and rub with taco seasoning.

2. Coat slow-cooker with nonstick cooking spray; place steak in slow-cooker.

3. Top with onion, chilies, and vinegar.

4. Cover and cook on LOW for 6–8 hours or until meat is tender.

5. Remove steak to cutting board and cool slightly; use two forks to shred the steak.

6. Return to slow-cooker and heat through.

7. Spoon about ½ C. of the meat mixture down the center of each tortilla. Top with cheese, tomato, and sour cream. Fold ends and sides over filling; serve.

Makes 4 servings.

Ingredients

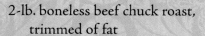

2-lb. boneless beef chuck roast, trimmed of fat

1 garlic clove, crushed

1 C. beef broth

1 small onion, chopped

½ tsp. chili powder

½ tsp. ground cumin

2 Tbsp. chopped fresh cilantro

½ tsp. salt

1 16-oz. can refried beans, heated

6–8 12-inch flour tortillas, warmed

BEEF AND BEAN BURRITOS

1. In slow-cooker, combine meat, garlic, broth, onion, chili powder, cumin, cilantro, and salt.

2. Cover and cook on LOW for 6–8 hours or until meat is very tender.

3. Remove meat from slow-cooker; use two forks to shred beef.

4. Combine shredded beef with ¾ C. cooking juices.

5. Spread refried beans on warm tortillas. Top with shredded beef. Fold over sides of tortilla and roll up. Serve warm.

Makes 6–8 servings.

BEEF AND BEAN ENCHILADAS

1. In a nonstick skillet, brown beef, onion, and green pepper.

2. Add remaining ingredients except cheeses and tortillas. Bring to a boil.

3. Reduce heat; cover and simmer for 10 minutes.

4. In a medium bowl, combine cheeses.

5. In slow-cooker, layer about ¾ C. beef mixture, one tortilla, and about ¼ C. cheese. Repeat layers until all ingredients are used.

6. Cover and cook on LOW for 4–6 hours.

Makes 6 servings.

Note: Round slow-cookers work well with this recipe because they are the perfect size for the tortillas.

Ingredients

1 lb. lean ground beef

½ C. chopped onion

½ C. chopped green bell pepper

1 16-oz. can pinto beans, rinsed and drained

1 10-oz. can Rotel® tomatoes

1 C. water

1 tsp. chili powder

1 16-oz. can black beans, rinsed and drained

½ tsp. ground cumin

½ tsp. salt

¼ tsp. black pepper

Dash of Tabasco sauce

1 C. shredded sharp cheddar cheese

1 C. shredded Monterey Jack cheese

6 6-inch flour tortillas

MEXICAN LASAGNA

1. In a medium bowl, mix beef, tomato sauce, and taco seasoning.

2. Spread refried beans on bottom of slow-cooker.

3. Layer ⅓ meat sauce, ⅓ cheese, and ⅓ tortilla pieces; repeat two more times.

4. Cover and cook on LOW for 4 hours.

Makes 4 servings.

Ingredients

½ lb. lean ground beef, browned and drained

1 8-oz. can tomato sauce

½ env. taco seasoning (.75 oz.)

1 C. refried beans

2 C. shredded cheddar cheese

4 10-inch flour or corn tortillas, cut into 1-inch squares

Ingredients

3 potatoes, peeled and quartered

1 onion, chopped

6 carrots, peeled and sliced into 1-inch pieces

2 lbs. boneless round steak

1 1-oz. env. dry onion soup mix

1 10¾-oz. can condensed cream of mushroom soup

¾ C. water

TENDER AND YUMMY ROUND STEAK

1. Place the potatoes, onion, and carrots in the bottom of slow-cooker.

2. Cut steak into six pieces; arrange meat on top of vegetables.

3. In a mixing bowl, combine the onion soup mix, soup, and water; pour over beef.

4. Cover and cook on LOW for 7–8 hours.

Makes 6 servings.

Ingredients

2- to 2½-lb. boneless beef chuck roast

½ env. dry onion soup mix (.5 oz.)

1 10¾-oz. can cream of mushroom soup

1 4-oz. can of mushrooms, drained

POT ROAST WITH CREAMY MUSHROOM SAUCE

1. Place roast in slow-cooker. Press the soup mix on all sides of the roast.

2. Top with mushroom soup and mushrooms.

3. Cover and cook on HIGH for 1 hour and then on LOW for 6–8 hours or until meat is tender.

Makes 6–8 servings.

TEXAS-STYLE BEEF BRISKET

1. In a large resealable plastic bag, combine Worcestershire sauce, chili powder, bay leaves, garlic, black pepper, and liquid smoke.

2. Cut visible fat off the brisket. Cut brisket in half and place in bag; rub the seasoning mixture all over the meat and refrigerate overnight.

3. The next day, place the beef in the slow-cooker and pour the beef broth over the meat.

4. Cover and cook on LOW for 6–8 hours or until tender.

5. Cut the meat into thin slices and serve with your favorite barbecue sauce.

Makes 12 servings.

Ingredients

3 Tbsp. Worcestershire sauce

1 Tbsp. chili powder

2 bay leaves

2 garlic cloves, minced

1 tsp. black pepper

1 tsp. liquid smoke

6 lbs. beef brisket

½ C. beef broth

ITALIAN SEASONED ROAST BEEF

1. Rub the roast with the Italian dressing mix.

2. In a skillet, heat the oil; brown the roast for 1–2 minutes on each side.

3. Place roast in slow-cooker.

4. Cover and cook on LOW for 7–8 hours.

5. Remove roast and slice. Make gravy out of the drippings, if desired.

Makes 4–6 servings.

Ingredients

1- to 2-lb. boneless beef chuck roast

1 .7-oz. env. dry Italian dressing mix

1 Tbsp. canola oil

1 C. beef broth

Ingredients

1 garlic clove, minced

1 tsp. lemon pepper

½ tsp. dried basil

1- to 2-lb. boneless beef chuck roast

1 C. beef broth

1 C. water

3 red potatoes, cut into small cubes

2 Tbsp. cornstarch dissolved in 2 Tbsp. water

LEMON-HERBED POT ROAST

1. Combine garlic, lemon pepper, and basil; press onto all sides of beef.

2. Pour broth and water into slow-cooker. Place roast in slow-cooker.

3. Place potatoes around the meat. Sprinkle lightly with additional lemon pepper.

4. Cover and cook on HIGH for 1 hour. Turn to LOW and cook for an additional 5–6 hours.

5. Transfer meat and potatoes to a serving platter.

6. Pour liquid from slow-cooker into a saucepan and heat to a boil. Add cornstarch mixture and whisk to make gravy. Serve gravy over roast and potatoes.

Makes 4–6 servings.

Ingredients

Baby carrots (as many as you desire)

4 potatoes, peeled and cubed

1½-lb. boneless beef chuck roast

Salt and pepper to taste

1 10¾-oz. can cream of mushroom soup

2 minute prep

SLOW-COOKER ROAST BEEF DINNER

1. Place carrots and potatoes on bottom of slow-cooker.

2. Place roast on top of veggies; season with salt and pepper.

3. Pour cream of mushroom soup over top of roast.

4. Cover and cook on LOW for 6–8 hours or until meat is tender.

Makes 4 servings.

FRENCH DIP

1. Place roast in slow-cooker. Add water, soy sauce, and seasonings.
2. Cover and cook on LOW for 6–8 hours.
3. Remove meat from broth and thinly slice or shred.
4. Strain broth and skim off fat; pour broth into small cups for dipping.
5. Serve sliced or shredded beef on rolls; dip sandwiches in broth.

Makes 12 servings.

Ingredients

2-lb. beef top round roast, trimmed of visible fat

3 C. water

1 C. soy sauce

1 tsp. dried rosemary

1 tsp. dried thyme

1 tsp. garlic powder

1 bay leaf

GARLIC HERB ROAST AND RED POTATOES

1. Place the quartered potatoes in the bottom of the slow-cooker.

2. In a dish, combine garlic salt, garlic powder, basil, thyme, parsley, and garlic. Roll the roast in the herbs until well coated.

3. In a skillet, heat the oil until hot; place the roast in the skillet and sear all sides of the meat, cooking about 1 minute on each side. Place the roast in the slow-cooker on top of the potatoes.

4. Cover and cook on LOW for 6–8 hours, until meat is fork-tender.

Makes 4 servings.

Ingredients

4 medium red potatoes, quartered

½ tsp. garlic salt

1 tsp. garlic powder

1 tsp. dried basil leaves

1 tsp. dried thyme leaves

1 tsp. dried parsley leaves

2 cloves fresh garlic, minced

1-lb. rump roast

1 tsp. canola oil

BEEF GYROS

1. Place beef in slow-cooker.

2. In a small bowl, mix oil, lemon juice, garlic, oregano, salt, and pepper.

3. Pour mixture over beef, turning beef to coat.

4. Cover and cook on LOW for 4–6 hours, until meat is tender.

5. Warm pitas as package directs.

6. Stuff pitas with sliced meat, Yogurt-Dill Sauce (below), and toppings.

Yogurt-Dill Sauce
1 C. plain Greek yogurt, 1 C. diced seedless cucumber, 1 Tbsp. dill, ¼ tsp. salt
Combine all ingredients; mix well.

Makes 6 servings.

Ingredients

2-lb. boneless beef chuck steak, sliced ¼-inch thick

¼ C. olive oil

2 Tbsp. lemon juice

1 Tbsp. minced garlic

1 tsp. dried oregano

½ tsp. salt

¼ tsp. pepper

Pita bread

Yogurt-Dill Sauce (see recipe at left)

Toppings: lettuce, tomatoes, onions

Ingredients

4 lbs. boneless beef chuck roast, cut into ½-inch cubes

1½ C. chopped onion

2 garlic cloves, minced

1 C. beef broth

1 6-oz. can tomato paste

2 tsp. salt

2 tsp. dried oregano

1 tsp. dried basil

½ tsp. dried rosemary

Dash of pepper

Pita bread

Toppings:

Shredded lettuce

Diced tomato

Diced cucumber

8 oz. plain yogurt

MEDITERRANEAN SANDWICHES

1. In slow-cooker, combine meat, onion, garlic, broth, tomato paste, salt, oregano, basil, rosemary, and dash of pepper. Mix well.

2. Cover and cook on LOW for 6–8 hours.

3. Split each pita bread to make a pocket; fill each with meat mixture and desired toppings.

Makes 10–16 sandwiches.

HEALTHY STUFFED PEPPERS

1. In a medium bowl, combine ground beef, garlic powder, onion powder, rice, and 1 can of tomatoes; mix well.

2. Stuff mixture into cored bell peppers. Arrange bell peppers in slow-cooker.

3. Cover and cook on LOW for 6–8 hours or on HIGH for 3–4 hours.

4. To serve, cut peppers in half. Heat tomatoes from second can and spoon on top of the pepper halves. (It's important to cut the stuffed peppers in half before spooning the tomatoes over them, because the centers will be a little dry without the added juice.)

Makes 8 servings.

Ingredients

1 lb. extra-lean ground beef

¾ tsp. garlic powder

½ tsp. onion powder

2 C. instant brown rice

2 14-oz. cans stewed or diced tomatoes, undrained

4 large green bell peppers, cored and seeded

DIPPING ROAST BEEF SLIDERS

1. Place roast in slow-cooker. Top with soup, juice from banana pepper rings, and Worcestershire sauce. Store banana peppers in refrigerator for later.

2. Cover and cook on LOW for 6–8 hours, or until beef is very tender.

3. Remove beef from slow-cooker to a cutting board and use two forks to shred. Pour the liquid from the slow-cooker into individual serving cups.

4. Serve the beef on top of the toasted buns. Top with the banana peppers and the provolone cheese (if desired). Dip in the liquid.

Makes 6–8 servings.

2 minute prep

ALL DAY

Ingredients

2-lb. boneless beef chuck roast, trimmed of fat

1 10¾-oz. can condensed French onion soup

1 8-oz. jar pickled banana pepper rings

2 Tbsp. Worcestershire sauce

Sliced provolone cheese (optional)

Mini buns, toasted

Ingredients

3-lb. boneless beef chuck roast

5 garlic cloves

1 16-oz. jar sliced pepperoncini peppers

2 tsp. fresh rosemary

2 tsp. fresh thyme

Sandwich bread and cheese of your choice

PEPPERONCINI BEEF SANDWICHES

1. Cut 5 small slits in roast, spacing the slits all around the roast. Tuck 1 clove of garlic into each slit.

2. Place roast in slow-cooker. Pour pepperoncinis, including the juice, over the roast. Sprinkle rosemary and thyme over the roast.

3. Cover and cook on LOW for 6–8 hours.

4. Slice roast and serve on sandwiches.

Makes 12 servings.

Ingredients

3-lb. boneless beef chuck roast

1 C. water

2 beef bouillon cubes or 2 tsp. beef bouillon granules

1 Tbsp. minced onion

1 15-oz. can tomato sauce

¼ C. brown sugar

¼ C. ketchup

¼ C. mustard

½ tsp. Worcestershire sauce

BARBECUED BEEF SANDWICHES

1. Place roast, water, and bouillon in slow-cooker.

2. Cover and cook on LOW for 6 hours or until very tender.

3. Remove beef to a cutting board and use two forks to shred meat; retain 1 C. of the juice from cooking. Return shredded beef and sauce to slow-cooker.

4. Add onion, tomato sauce, brown sugar, ketchup, mustard, and Worcestershire sauce to shredded meat in slow-cooker.

5. Cover and cook on LOW for 3 hours or on HIGH for 1½–2 hours.

6. Serve over hoagie buns.

Makes 12 servings.

CREAMY BALSAMIC RIBS

1. Place ribs in slow-cooker.

2. In a small bowl, mix dressing, garlic, and onion powder. Pour over the top of the ribs.

3. Cover and cook on LOW for 6–8 hours.

4. Serve with sauce.

Makes 3 servings.

Ingredients

1 lb. boneless beef country-style ribs

½ C. Ken's Creamy Balsamic Dressing

2 garlic cloves, minced

½ tsp. onion powder

SLOPPY JOES

1. In a medium skillet, cook beef over medium-high heat until no longer pink, stirring to break up meat. Drain fat and transfer beef to slow-cooker.

2. Add ketchup, mustard, and pork and beans. Stir to mix well.

3. Cover and cook on LOW for 4–6 hours.

4. Serve on buns.

Makes 6 servings.

Ingredients

2 lbs. lean ground beef

½ C. ketchup

¼ C. prepared yellow mustard

1 14-oz. can pork and beans

6 hamburger buns

Ingredients

5 C. barbecue sauce

¾ C. brown sugar

2 Tbsp. Cajun seasoning

1 Tbsp. garlic powder

1 Tbsp. onion powder

6 lbs. boneless beef country-style
   ribs

SWEET AND SPICY RIBS

1. In a medium bowl, mix barbecue sauce, brown sugar, Cajun seasoning, garlic powder, and onion powder. Remove 1 C. of mixture; refrigerate and reserve for dipping sauce.

2. Place ribs in large slow-cooker. Pour barbecue sauce mixture over ribs.

3. Cover and cook on LOW for 6–8 hours or until meat is tender.

4. Uncover; remove ribs. Skim fat from sauce and serve with reserved sauce.

Makes 10 servings.

Ingredients

2 lbs. lean ground beef

4 garlic cloves, minced

1 14-oz. can undrained diced
   tomatoes

1 10-oz. can condensed tomato soup

1 tsp. dried basil

½ tsp. salt

Dash of pepper

6 potatoes

1 16-oz. jar Alfredo sauce

1 14-oz. tub refrigerated pesto sauce

½ C. grated Parmesan cheese

SLOW-COOKER PESTO AND BEEF CASSEROLE

1. In large skillet, cook ground beef with garlic, stirring to break up beef, until beef is thoroughly cooked. Drain well.

2. Add tomatoes, tomato soup, basil, salt, and pepper. Bring to a simmer.

3. Slice potatoes ⅛-inch thick.

4. In medium bowl, combine Alfredo sauce, pesto, and Parmesan.

5. Layer half of beef mixture, half the potatoes, and half the Alfredo mixture in slow-cooker. Repeat layers, using all ingredients.

6. Cover and cook on LOW for 6–8 hours or until potatoes are tender.

Makes 8–10 servings.

CORNED BEEF AND CABBAGE

1. Lightly spray slow-cooker with nonstick cooking spray.

2. Layer potato slices, carrots, and celery on bottom of slow-cooker. Place corned beef on top of vegetables.

3. Slice cabbage into 8 wedges; arrange around meat. Sprinkle with the pepper and add water.

4. Cover and cook on LOW for 7–8 hours, until meat and vegetables are tender.

5. Slice and serve.

Makes 8 servings.

Ingredients

6–8 medium potatoes, peeled and cut into ½-inch slices

3 medium carrots, thinly sliced

2 celery ribs, thinly sliced

3-lb. corned beef brisket

1 head of cabbage (about 2 lbs.)

½ tsp. black pepper

1½ C. water

POULTRY DISHES

Sick of the same old chicken recipes? Try these delicious, easy poultry dinner recipes to keep your mealtime exciting and your family happy.

seasoned

sweet n sour

lettuce wraps Fajitas

turkey

taco Calzone

artichoke chicken lemon

curry casserole

rice

Parmesan

family dinner chicken a la king

tender

Ingredients

1 6-lb. bone-in turkey breast, thawed

1 1-oz. env. dry onion soup mix

3 Tbsp. butter

SLOW-COOKER TURKEY BREAST

1. Rinse the turkey breast and pat dry.

2. Cut off any excess skin, but leave the skin covering the breast.

3. Rub onion soup mix all over the outside of the turkey and under the skin.

4. Place butter in bottom of slow-cooker and let it melt for a couple of minutes. Then place turkey breast in slow-cooker.

5. Cover and cook on HIGH for 1 hour; turn heat to LOW and cook for 7 hours or until turkey breast comes to a temperature of 165 degrees.

6. Remove turkey from slow-cooker and let it sit for 10–15 minutes.

7. Use the drippings in the slow-cooker to make gravy.

Makes 8 servings.

Ingredients

4–8 oz. mushrooms, thinly sliced

1 C. Alfredo sauce

1¼ C. picante sauce, divided

2 garlic cloves, minced

1 Tbsp. quick-cooking tapioca

1 Tbsp. Italian salad dressing mix

Salt and pepper to taste

3–4 turkey thighs, skin removed, washed and patted dry

1 14-oz. can Great Northern beans

Hot, cooked noodles or rice

SAUCY TURKEY THIGHS

1. In the slow-cooker, combine mushrooms, Alfredo sauce, 1 C. picante sauce, garlic, tapioca, and salad dressing mix; stir to mix.

2. Salt and pepper the turkey and nestle into the slow-cooker.

3. Cover and cook on LOW for 4–6 hours.

4. Remove turkey thighs and tent loosely with foil.

5. Rinse and drain beans; puree in a blender or food processor.

6. Skim any fat off the top of the sauce in the slow-cooker.

7. Stir in as much bean puree as needed to thicken sauce; stir in additional ¼ C. picante sauce.

8. Serve sauce over turkey and noodles or rice.

Makes 4 servings.

WHOLE CHICKEN

1. Place chicken breast-side down in greased slow-cooker; add water.

2. Cover and cook on LOW for 6–8 hours or until chicken comes to a temperature of 165 degrees.

3. Remove meat from bones; pack cooked meat into plastic freezer bags and store in freezer to use in recipes that call for cooked chicken.

Makes 2–3 pints of cooked chicken.

Ingredients

1 large whole chicken, skin removed

1 C. water

CORNISH GAME HENS

1. Place onion slices in bottom of slow-cooker.

2. Mix garlic, lemon pepper, salt, and basil; rub all over the hens.

3. Place hens breast-side down on top of onion slices.

4. Cover and cook on LOW for about 4 hours. Discard onions and serve.

Makes 4 servings.

Ingredients

1 small onion, cut into thick slices

4 garlic cloves, minced

1 tsp. lemon pepper

½ tsp. kosher salt

½ tsp. dried basil

2 Cornish game hens, thawed, skin removed, and patted dry

Ingredients

2 lbs. boneless, skinless chicken thighs

1 1.25-oz. env. taco seasoning mix

1 15-oz. can pinto beans, kidney beans, or black beans, drained

1 14.5-oz. can diced tomatoes, undrained

1 4.5-oz. can chopped green chilies

2 Tbsp. lime juice

1 10-oz. bag tortilla chips

Optional Toppings: shredded cheese, sour cream, salsa, olives, fresh cilantro, guacamole, and lime wedges

SHREDDED CHICKEN NACHOS

1. Place chicken in slow-cooker and sprinkle with taco seasoning mix.

2. Top with beans, tomatoes, chilies, and lime juice.

3. Cover and cook on LOW for 4–6 hours.

4. Remove chicken from slow-cooker and place on cutting board.

5. Mash the beans in the slow-cooker.

6. Shred chicken with two forks; return chicken to slow-cooker and mix well.

7. To serve, spoon chicken mixture onto chips.

8. Top nachos with desired toppings.

Makes 12 servings.

Ingredients

1 8-oz. bottle zesty Italian dressing

1 Tbsp. chili powder

1 Tbsp. cumin

3 garlic cloves, minced

5 lbs. boneless, skinless chicken breasts

CAFÉ RIO CHICKEN

1. In a small bowl, mix Italian dressing, chili powder, cumin, and garlic.

2. Place chicken on bottom of a greased slow-cooker.

3. Pour dressing mixture over the top of chicken.

4. Cover and cook on LOW for 4–6 hours.

5. Remove chicken to a cutting board; use two forks to shred chicken. Reserve juice to pour over chicken when serving.

6. Serve chicken wrapped in tortillas or on top of salad.

Makes 15 servings.

CHICKEN AND BLACK BEANS

1. Place chicken breasts and thighs, salsa, and beans in slow-cooker.

2. Cover and cook on LOW for 4–6 hours.

3. Remove chicken to cutting board; sprinkle with garlic salt and pepper to taste.

3. Use two forks to shred chicken. Serve on warm tortillas with grated cheese, sour cream, lettuce, avocado, and squeeze of lime juice.

Makes 8 servings.

Ingredients

4 boneless, skinless chicken breast halves

4 boneless, skinless chicken thighs

2 C. salsa

2 14-oz. cans black beans or pinto beans

Garlic salt to taste

Pepper to taste

Tortillas

Toppings: cheese, sour cream, lettuce, avocado, lime juice

LAYERED CHICKEN ENCHILADAS

1. Lightly coat slow-cooker with cooking spray.

2. In a large bowl, combine all ingredients except tortilla strips.

3. On bottom of slow-cooker, layer half of tortilla strips then half of chicken mixture. Repeat layers.

4. Cover and cook on LOW for 3–5 hours.

Makes 6–8 servings.

Ingredients

4–6 chicken breasts, cooked and cubed

1 7-oz. can diced green chilies

1 C. sour cream

1 10¾-oz. can cream of chicken soup

1 10¾-oz. can cream of mushroom soup

1 14-oz. can Mexican stewed tomatoes

1 tsp. salt

1 tsp. chili powder

1 tsp. cumin

1 C. shredded cheese

5 10-inch flour tortillas, sliced oblong into 2-inch strips

Ingredients

3 frozen boneless, skinless chicken breast halves

3 thawed boneless, skinless chicken thighs

2½ C. chunky salsa

1 green pepper, thinly sliced

1 red pepper, thinly sliced

1 large onion, thinly sliced

Black beans (optional)

8 soft flour tortillas

Optional toppings: guacamole, sour cream, lettuce, cheese, salsa

Ingredients

1 small onion, minced

1½ Tbsp. chili powder

1 Tbsp. canola oil

2 garlic cloves, minced

1 tsp. ground coriander

1 tsp. cumin

½ C. salsa

1 tsp. sugar

8 oz. boneless, skinless chicken thighs (thawed)

8 oz. boneless, skinless chicken breasts (frozen)

2 tsp. lime juice

Salt and pepper to taste

Toppings: cheese, cilantro, and tomatoes

CHICKEN FAJITAS

1. Place chicken breasts and thighs, salsa, peppers, and onions in slow-cooker.

2. Cover and cook on LOW for 4–6 hours.

3. Just before serving, remove fajita mixture with a spoon and use two forks to shred chicken.

4. Add beans to mixture, if desired.

5. Place two rounded tablespoons of chicken and fajita mixture in each flour tortilla and top with desired toppings. Fold and roll.

Makes 8 servings.

CHICKEN TACO FILLING

1. In a microwave-safe bowl, combine onion, chili powder, oil, garlic, coriander, and cumin. Cook in microwave for about 3 minutes, stirring every minute, until onion is tender. Pour into slow-cooker.

2. Stir in salsa and sugar.

3. Add the chicken; stir to coat.

4. Cover and cook on LOW for 4–6 hours.

5. Remove cover and shred chicken with two forks. Stir in the lime juice and salt and pepper to taste.

6. Serve in tortillas with cheese, cilantro, and tomatoes.

Makes 4 servings.

Ingredients

½ medium onion, chopped

1 Tbsp. chili powder

3 garlic cloves, minced

1 tsp. dried oregano

1 Tbsp. canola or vegetable oil

1 8-oz. can tomato sauce

1 tsp. brown sugar

1 piece of bread

2 Tbsp. milk

1 lb. Gold'n Plump® ground chicken (90/10)

¼ tsp. salt

⅛ tsp. pepper

Salt and pepper to taste

Lime juice to taste

Tortillas

Toppings: cheese, cilantro, avocado, tomatoes, sour cream

GROUND CHICKEN TACO FILLING

1. In a microwave-safe bowl, combine onion, chili powder, garlic, oregano, and oil. Microwave for 4–5 minutes, stirring every minute, until onion is soft. Transfer to the slow-cooker.

2. Stir in tomato sauce and brown sugar.

3. In a separate bowl, mash the bread and milk into a paste. Add the ground chicken, ¼ tsp. salt, and ⅛ tsp. pepper. Mix but do not overstir.

4. Add chicken mixture to slow-cooker and stir to combine.

5. Cover and cook on LOW for 4 hours or on HIGH for 2 hours.

6. Salt and pepper to taste. Add lime juice to taste.

7. Place chicken filling on tortillas and top with desired toppings. Wrap and serve.

Makes 4 tacos.

TOMATILLO CHICKEN FILLING

1. Pat chicken breasts and thighs dry and season with salt and pepper. Place in slow-cooker.

2. In a microwave-safe bowl, combine onion, jalapeño, poblano, garlic, oregano, cumin, and oil; microwave for 4–5 minutes, stirring every minute, until onion is soft. Transfer to slow-cooker. Add the tomatillos.

3. Cover and cook on LOW for 4–6 hours.

4. Remove chicken and use two forks to shred.

5. Strain the liquid in the slow-cooker into a bowl. Puree the strained solids in a blender. Add puree to the chicken. Add cumin, salt, and pepper to taste; stir in fresh lime juice. If needed, stir in some of the strained liquid.

6. Serve the filling wrapped up in tortillas with sour cream, cilantro, lettuce, cheese, tomatoes, and other toppings of your choice.

Makes 4–5 servings.

cook's FAV.

Ingredients

2 chicken breast halves

3 boneless, skinless chicken thighs, trimmed of fat

1 jalapeño, halved lenthwise, stem and seeds removed, and chopped

1 poblano, stem and seeds removed, and chopped coarsely

3 garlic cloves, minced

½ tsp. dried oregano

½ tsp. ground cumin

2 Tbsp. canola or vegetable oil

8–10 medium tomatillos, husks removed, rinsed well, and halved

Cumin to taste

Salt and pepper to taste

2 tsp. fresh lime juice

Toppings: sour cream, cilantro, lettuce, cheese, tomatoes

Ingredients

½ lb. boneless, skinless chicken breasts

½ lb. boneless, skinless chicken thighs

1 10-oz. can mild green enchilada sauce

1 4-oz. can diced green chilies

½ tsp. cumin

⅛ tsp. chili powder

1 Tbsp. lime juice

3 garlic cloves, minced

Toppings: cheese, cilantro, tomatoes, sour cream, beans

Ingredients

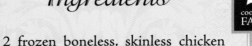

2 frozen boneless, skinless chicken breast halves

2 thawed boneless, skinless chicken thighs

½ C. chicken broth

1 C. salsa or picante sauce

1 C. frozen corn

1 15-oz. can black beans, drained and rinsed

1 1.25-oz. env. taco seasoning

½ C. sour cream

1 Tbsp. cornstarch

1 Tbsp. water

Tortillas

Grated cheddar cheese

EASY CHICKEN BURRITOS

1. Place chicken breasts and thighs in bottom of slow-cooker.

2. Mix remaining ingredients except toppings and pour over the top of the chicken.

3. Cover and cook on LOW for 4–6 hours.

4. Shred chicken with two forks and stir well to combine with the sauce.

5. Salt and pepper to taste. Serve on top of tortillas with cheese, cilantro, tomatoes, sour cream, beans, and any other toppings you desire.

Makes 4 servings.

CREAMY BLACK BEAN SALSA CHICKEN

1. Place the chicken breasts and thighs in the slow-cooker and cover with the broth, salsa, corn, beans, and taco seasoning.

2. Cover and cook on LOW for 4–6 hours.

3. Remove the chicken and either shred it or cut it up into bite-size pieces.

4. Stir in the sour cream.

5. In a small bowl, combine the cornstarch and water; stir until smooth. Stir cornstarch mixture into the slow-cooker mixture.

6. Put the chicken back into the slow-cooker.

7. Keep the lid off; turn to HIGH and let the mixture thicken for about 30 minutes.

8. Spoon the chicken mixture over tortillas and sprinkle with cheese.

Make 4–6 servings.

HERBED TOMATO ARTICHOKE CHICKEN

1. In a small microwave-safe bowl, combine the onions, garlic, and 2 Tbsp. chicken broth. Cook in microwave for 4–5 minutes, stirring every minute, until the onions are soft. Pour into the slow-cooker.

2. Put chicken, tomatoes, artichoke hearts, remaining chicken broth, tapioca, curry powder, parsley flakes, basil, thyme, salt, and black pepper in the slow-cooker. Stir to combine.

3. Cover and cook on LOW for 4–6 hours.

4. Use two forks to break the chicken up into large pieces.

5. Serve the chicken and sauce over fettuccine noodles.

Makes 4 servings.

⅓ C. chopped onion

3 garlic cloves, minced

½ C. chicken broth, divided

¾ lb. boneless, skinless chicken thighs

1 14-oz. can diced tomatoes, drained

1 14-oz. can artichoke hearts in water, drained

3 Tbsp. quick-cooking tapioca

2 tsp. curry powder

1 tsp. dried parsley flakes

1 tsp. basil

1 tsp. thyme

¼ tsp. salt

¼ tsp. black pepper

Cooked fettuccine noodles

LIME CHICKEN AND PEPPERS

1. Cut each chicken thigh and breast into 4 pieces. Put chicken in slow-cooker.

2. Combine garlic, broth, 2 Tbsp. lime juice, soy sauce, chicken, red onion, and pepper strips in slow-cooker. Stir to coat chicken.

3. Cover and cook on LOW for 3–4 hours.

4. In a large skillet, melt butter over low heat. Sprinkle in ¼ C. flour and stir with wire whisk. Slowly add in half-and-half or milk and stir with whisk.

5. Remove about ½ C. liquid from the slow-cooker and add to the skillet. Whisk in remaining ¼ C. flour and stir until creamy.

6. Add 2 Tbsp. lime juice to the skillet.

7. Pour the rest of the contents from the slow-cooker into the skillet and stir to combine. Stir in cooked pasta until it is all coated with sauce.

8. Garnish with cilantro and serve.

Makes 4–6 servings.

Ingredients

2 boneless, skinless chicken thighs

2 boneless, skinless chicken breast halves

2 garlic cloves, minced

½ C. chicken broth

4 Tbsp. lime juice, divided

3 Tbsp. soy sauce

½ medium red onion, finely diced

1 each red, green, orange, and yellow pepper, cut into long strips

¼ C. butter

½ C. flour, divided

1 C. half-and-half (or whole milk)

1 lb. spinach fettuccine noodles, cooked and drained

Cilantro for garnish

Ingredients

1 10-oz. can green enchilada sauce

1 4-oz. can chopped green chilies

1 tsp. dried oregano

½ tsp. garlic salt

½ tsp. ground cumin

1 Tbsp. quick-cooking tapioca

6 chicken drumsticks, skin removed

1 Tbsp. cornstarch

1 Tbsp. cold water

Hot, cooked rice

MEXICAN DRUMSTICKS

1. In a medium bowl, combine enchilada sauce, chilies, oregano, garlic salt, cumin, and tapioca.

2. Place drumsticks in slow-cooker; top with enchilada sauce mixture.

3. Cover and cook on LOW for 4–6 hours.

4. Remove chicken and keep warm.

5. Strain sauce into a saucepan. Combine the cornstarch and water and stir until smooth; stir into the pan. Bring to a boil; cook and stir for 2 minutes or until sauce is thickened.

6. Serve sauce with chicken and rice.

Makes 6 servings.

OOEY GOOEY MEXICAN CHICKEN

1. Combine chicken, soups, salsa, beans, chilies, chili powder, and cumin in slow-cooker.

2. Cover and cook on LOW for 3–4 hours.

3. Using two forks, shred the chicken.

4. Stir the pepper and cheese into the chicken mixture.

5. Serve with tortilla chips or flour tortillas.

Makes 6 servings.

Ingredients

3 chicken breasts

1 10¾-oz. can cream of chicken soup

1 10¾-oz. can cream of mushroom soup

1 C. salsa

1 15-oz. can black beans, drained and rinsed

1 4-oz. can diced green chilies

1 tsp. chili powder

1 tsp. cumin

¼ tsp. pepper

1½ C. shredded Monterey Jack cheese

Tortilla chips or flour tortillas

SLOW-COOKER MEXICAN CHICKEN

1. Spray slow-cooker with nonstick cooking spray and put corn in bottom of slow-cooker. Place chicken on top of corn. Sprinkle chicken with taco seasoning. Pour in salsa, green chilies, and beans.

2. Cover and cook on LOW for 4–6 hours.

3. Stir mixture, breaking apart chicken so it is shredded. Add cilantro. Use a slotted spoon to spoon mixture over tortillas.

Makes 4 servings.

Ingredients

1¼ C. frozen corn

2 frozen boneless, skinless chicken breasts

½ env. taco seasoning (.75 oz.)

1 12-oz. jar salsa

1 4-oz. can diced green chilies

1 14-oz. can black beans, rinsed and drained

Chopped fresh cilantro, to taste

Tortillas

Ingredients

1 10¾-oz. can cream of chicken soup

¼ C. water

2 Tbsp. lemon juice

1 tsp. Dijon-style mustard

¾ tsp. garlic powder

4 boneless, skinless chicken thighs

Noodles, potatoes, or rice

Grated Parmesan cheese

Ingredients

1 lb. boneless, skinless chicken thighs, trimmed of fat and cut into ¾-inch pieces

1 14-oz. can artichokes, drained and quartered

1 16-oz. jar Alfredo sauce

½ C. chicken broth

1 Tbsp. quick-cooking tapioca

½ C. chopped tomatoes

1 4-oz. can mushrooms, drained, or 1 C. fresh button mushrooms, sliced

Cooked noodles or rice

2 Tbsp. shredded Parmesan cheese

LEMON CREAMY CHICKEN

1. In slow-cooker, mix soup, water, lemon juice, mustard, and garlic powder. Add chicken and turn to coat.

2. Cover and cook on LOW for 4–6 hours or until chicken is done.

3. Using two forks, break up the chicken into large chunks.

4. Serve chicken and sauce over noodles, potatoes, or rice. Sprinkle with cheese.

Makes 4 servings.

CHICKEN AND NOODLES ALFREDO

1. In slow-cooker, mix chicken, artichokes, Alfredo sauce, broth, and tapioca.

2. Cover and cook on LOW for 3–5 hours.

3. About 30 minutes before serving, stir in tomatoes and mushrooms. Increase heat to HIGH. Cover; cook 30 minutes longer.

4. Serve chicken and sauce over noodles or rice. Sprinkle cheese over individual servings.

Makes 4 servings.

CHEESY CHICKEN NOODLES

1. Place chicken in slow-cooker.

2. In a medium bowl, combine soup, milk, onion, and basil; pour over chicken.

3. Cover and cook on LOW for 3–5 hours.

4. Add mushrooms and sour cream and let heat through. Salt and pepper to taste.

5. Serve over hot, cooked noodles or rice.

Makes 6 servings.

Ingredients

6 boneless, skinless chicken breast halves

2 10¾-oz. cans broccoli cheese soup

1 14-oz. can evaporated milk

½ C. dried minced onion

½ tsp. dried basil

1 4-oz. can mushrooms, drained

½ C. sour cream

Salt and pepper to taste

Hot, cooked noodles or rice

CHICKEN AND RICE

1. In slow-cooker, combine soup, water, rice, paprika, and pepper.

2. Salt and pepper the chicken thighs lightly and place on top of rice mixture.

3. Sprinkle with additional paprika and pepper.

4. Cover and cook on LOW for 4–6 hours until rice is soft and fluffy.

Makes 4 servings.

Ingredients

1 10¾-oz. can cream of mushroom soup

1 C. water

¾ C. long-grain brown rice

¼ tsp. paprika

¼ tsp. pepper

Salt and pepper to taste

4 bone-in chicken thighs, skin removed

Ingredients

1½ C. picante sauce

3 Tbsp. brown sugar

1 Tbsp. Dijon mustard

4 frozen boneless, skinless chicken breast halves

Tortillas or hot, cooked rice

2 minute prep

PICANTE SAUCE CHICKEN

1. In a small bowl, mix picante sauce, sugar, and mustard.

2. Place chicken in bottom of slow-cooker and pour sauce over chicken.

3. Cover and cook on LOW for 3–4 hours.

4. Use two forks to shred the chicken; serve wrapped in tortillas or over rice.

Makes 4–6 servings.

Ingredients

1 onion, finely diced

3 garlic cloves, minced

1 Tbsp. tomato paste

1 tsp. canola oil

2 red bell peppers, chopped

3 lbs. chicken tenders, cut in half

1 8-oz. pkg. cream cheese, cut into cubes

2 16-oz. jars Alfredo sauce

1 C. evaporated milk

1 10¾-oz. can cream of chicken soup

1 tsp. dried basil leaves

⅛ tsp. pepper

1 Tbsp. quick-cooking tapioca

Hot, cooked noodles, mashed potatoes, biscuits, or rice

CHICKEN A LA KING

1. In a microwave-safe bowl, combine onion, garlic, tomato paste, and oil. Cook in microwave on high for 4–5 minutes, stirring every minute, until the onions are soft.

2. Put onion mixture, bell peppers, and chicken in slow-cooker.

3. In food processor or blender, combine cream cheese with Alfredo sauce and evaporated milk; blend until combined. Pour into large bowl and add cream of chicken soup, basil, pepper, and tapioca. Mix well. Pour sauce into slow-cooker.

4. Cover and cook on LOW for 3–4 hours or until chicken is tender. Salt and pepper to taste. Serve over hot, cooked noodles, potatoes, biscuits, or rice.

Makes 8–10 servings.

Ingredients

1 onion, diced

4 garlic cloves, minced

1 tsp. dried thyme leaves

1 Tbsp. canola oil

8 boneless, skinless chicken breast halves or chicken thighs

1 tsp. salt

⅛ tsp. pepper

8 thin slices of ham

1 16-oz. jar Alfredo sauce

1 10¾-oz. can cream of chicken soup

2 C. shredded Swiss cheese

Hot, cooked rice

Ingredients

6 small boneless, skinless chicken breasts halves, thawed and patted dry

6 slices of ham

6 slices of mozzarella or Swiss cheese

Garlic salt

1 10¾-oz. can cream of chicken soup

½ C. sour cream

¼ C. all-purpose flour

Hot, cooked rice

CHICKEN CORDON BLEU

1. In a microwaves-safe bowl, combine onion, garlic, thyme, and canola oil. Cook in microwave on high for 4–5 minutes, stirring every minute, until onions are soft.

2. Sprinkle chicken with salt and pepper. Wrap a slice of ham around each piece of chicken and secure with toothpicks. Place in bottom of slow-cooker.

3. In a medium bowl, combine Alfredo sauce, cream of chicken soup, onion mixture, and Swiss cheese. Pour over the chicken.

4. Cover and cook on LOW for 4–6 hours (less time for chicken breasts) or until chicken is thoroughly cooked.

5. Serve chicken and sauce with rice.

Makes 8 servings.

EASY CORDON BLEU

1. Slice chicken breast halves almost in half and place ham, cheese, and a sprinkle of garlic salt inside. Close and secure with a toothpick. Place chicken in bottom of slow-cooker.

2. In a small bowl, whisk the soup, sour cream, and flour. Pour soup mixture over the top of the chicken.

3. Cover and cook on LOW for 3–5 hours.

4. Serve chicken and sauce with hot, cooked rice.

Makes 6 servings.

LOW-FAT CHICKEN STROGANOFF

1. Spray slow-cooker with nonstick cooking spray.

2. Place chicken, chicken soup, sour cream, onion, bouillon, and onion powder in slow-cooker and mix until combined.

3. Cover and cook on LOW for 3–4 hours.

4. Serve over hot, cooked egg noodles.

Makes 6 servings.

Ingredients

1½ lbs. boneless, skinless chicken breasts, cut into 1-inch pieces

1 10¾-oz. can low-fat cream of chicken soup

2 C. non-fat sour cream

¼ C. instant minced onion

2 Tbsp. chicken bouillon granules

½ tsp. onion powder

3 C. cooked egg noodles

CHICKEN STROGANOFF

1. Combine the chicken, onion, mushrooms, soup, and tomato sauce in slow-cooker.

2. Cover and cook on LOW for 4–6 hours.

3. Add parsley, sour cream, and salt and pepper; stir and turn to HIGH. Let the slow-cooker sit without a lid for 10–15 minutes.

4. Serve over noodles or rice.

Makes 4–6 servings.

Ingredients

1½ lbs. boneless, skinless chicken thighs (not breasts), trimmed of fat and cut into 1-inch cubes

1 Tbsp. dehydrated onion or ¼ C. chopped onion

1 4-oz. can mushrooms, drained

1 10¾-oz. can cream of chicken soup

1 8-oz. can tomato sauce

2 tsp. dried parsley

½ C. sour cream

Salt and pepper to taste

Hot, cooked noodles or rice

Ingredients

12 garlic cloves, minced

1 medium onion, chopped

1 Tbsp. olive oil

1 14-oz. can artichoke hearts, drained and coarsely chopped

1 red pepper, cut into strips

½ C. chicken broth

1 Tbsp. quick-cooking tapioca

1 tsp. finely shredded lemon peel

½ tsp. ground black pepper

Salt and pepper to taste

1½ lbs. boneless, skinless thighs, trimmed of fat and patted dry

4 C. hot, cooked brown rice

CHICKEN WITH GARLIC, PEPPERS, AND ARTICHOKES

1. In a microwave-safe bowl, combine garlic, onion, and oil. Cook on high for 4–5 minutes, stirring every minute, until onions are softened. Pour into slow-cooker.

2. Add the artichoke hearts, red pepper, chicken broth, tapioca, lemon peel, and black pepper to slow-cooker. Salt and pepper the chicken and nestle into the slow-cooker.

3. Cover and cook on LOW for 4–6 hours.

4. Using two forks, break up chicken into large chunks.

5. Serve chicken and veggies with rice.

Makes 6 servings.

Ingredients

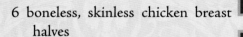

6 boneless, skinless chicken breast halves

¼ C. butter

1 .7-oz. env. Italian dressing mix

1 8-oz. pkg. cream cheese

1 10¾-oz. can cream of chicken soup

Hot, cooked rice

2 minute prep

★ cook's FAV.

CREAMY CHICKEN

1. Place chicken and butter in slow-cooker. Sprinkle with Italian dressing mix.

2. Cover and cook on LOW for 3–4 hours.

3. When ready to serve, add cream cheese and soup. Stir in until creamy. Serve over rice.

Makes 6 servings.

CREAMY ARTICHOKE CHICKEN

1. In a saucepan, combine water, Shirley J® Whisk Bliss, and Shirley J® Pizza and Pasta Seasoning Mix. Whisk until smooth. Bring to a boil over medium heat. Remove from heat and stir in the Parmesan cheese.

2. Place chicken, artichoke hearts, mushrooms, and sauce into slow-cooker. Stir to combine.

3. Cover and cook on LOW for 3–5 hours.

4. Half an hour before serving, add the tomatoes. Cover and cook on LOW until ready to serve. Serve over noodles, rice, or mashed potatoes.

Makes 6 servings.

2 C. water

½ C. Shirley J® Whisk Bliss

1 Tbsp. Shirley J® Pizza and Pasta Seasoning Mix

¼ C. Parmesan cheese

1–2 lbs. boneless, skinless chicken thighs, cut into ¾-inch pieces

1 14-oz. can artichoke hearts, drained

1 4-oz. can mushrooms, drained

½ C. chopped fresh tomatoes

Cooked noodles, rice, or mashed potatoes

CREAMY CHICKEN AND MUSHROOMS

1. Combine chicken and mushrooms in slow-cooker and sprinkle Ranch dressing mix over the top.

2. Dissolve bouillon cube in boiling water; pour over chicken. Make sure chicken is completely covered by liquid.

3. Cover and cook on LOW for 3–4 hours.

4. Stir in soup and cream cheese. Stir until melted and warmed. Serve over rice.

Makes 4 servings.

Ingredients

1½ lbs. chicken tenders or boneless skinless chicken breasts, cut into bite-size pieces

1 4-oz. can of mushrooms, drained

1 1-oz. env. Ranch dressing mix

1 chicken bouillon cube

1 C. boiling water

1 10¾-oz. can cream of chicken soup

1 8-oz. pkg. cream cheese

Hot, cooked rice

CHICKEN AND MUSHROOMS

1. In a microwave-safe bowl, combine the onion, garlic, oil, tomato paste, and thyme; cook for 3–4 minutes, stirring every minute, until onions are tender. Pour into slow-cooker.

2. Sprinkle the chicken with salt and pepper to taste. Stir the chicken, mushrooms, broth, vinegar, and tapioca into the slow-cooker.

3. Cover and cook on LOW for 4–6 hours.

4. Remove chicken; use two forks to break chicken into large pieces.

5. Remove fat from surface of sauce with a large spoon.

6. Put the chicken back into the slow-cooker. Add the milk, cheese, and parsley.

7. Salt and pepper to taste and serve over rice or pasta.

Makes 4 servings.

Ingredients

1 onion, minced

6 garlic cloves, minced

1 Tbsp. olive oil

1 Tbsp. tomato paste

1 tsp. dried thyme

1½ lbs. boneless, skinless chicken thighs, trimmed of fat

Salt and pepper to taste

1 lb. white mushrooms, thinly sliced

2 C. chicken broth

2 Tbsp. white wine vinegar

2 Tbsp. quick-cooking tapioca

¼ C. evaporated milk

½ C. Parmesan cheese

1 Tbsp. dried parsley flakes

Salt and pepper to taste

Hot, cooked rice or pasta

Ingredients

6 boneless, skinless chicken thighs, trimmed of fat

Salt and pepper to taste

1½ C. chopped fresh mushrooms

2 Tbsp. canola oil

1 small onion, diced

½ tsp. dried thyme

¼ tsp. salt

4 garlic cloves, minced

¼ C. flour

2 Tbsp. white wine vinegar

1½ C. chicken broth

2 Tbsp. soy sauce

2 bay leaves

1 Tbsp. quick-cooking tapioca

1½ tsp. dried tarragon

½ C. evaporated milk

Hot, cooked rice or noodles

MUSHROOM TARRAGON CHICKEN

1. Pat chicken dry and season with salt and pepper. Place in bottom of slow-cooker.

2. In a microwave-safe bowl, combine mushrooms, oil, onion, thyme, salt, garlic, and flour. Cook for 3 minutes, stirring every minute. Stir in vinegar, broth, soy sauce, bay leaves, and tapioca. Pour into the slow-cooker over the chicken.

3. Cover and cook on LOW for 4–6 hours.

4. Remove lid and use two forks to break chicken up into large pieces.

5. Stir in the tarragon and evaporated milk. Keep the lid off and turn to HIGH.

6. Cook for an additional 30 minutes on HIGH. Serve over rice or noodles.

Makes 6 servings.

ITALIAN CREAMY CHICKEN

1. Brush chicken with melted butter and place in slow-cooker. Sprinkle dry dressing mix over top of chicken.

2. Cover and cook on LOW for 3–4 hours.

3. About 45 minutes before serving, cut the cream cheese into small pieces. Stir cream cheese, soup, and onion into chicken. Cover and cook an additional 30 minutes.

4. Stir until creamy, salt and pepper to taste, and serve over rice or noodles.

Makes 8 servings.

Ingredients

3 lbs. boneless, skinless chicken breasts, cut into bite-size pieces

2 Tbsp. melted butter

1 .7-oz. env. dry Italian dressing mix

1 oz. cream cheese

1 10¾-oz. can cream of mushroom soup

1 Tbsp. finely diced onion

Salt and pepper to taste

Hot, cooked rice or noodles

SOUR CREAM MUSHROOM CHICKEN

1. Place chicken in bottom of slow-cooker. In a small bowl, combine soup mix and soup; pour over the top of the chicken.

2. Cover and cook on LOW for 3–4 hours.

3. Use two forks to break up the chicken into large pieces. Stir in sour cream and mushrooms and cook on LOW for an additional 30 minutes.

4. Serve over rice, noodles, or potatoes.

Makes 6 servings.

Ingredients

6 boneless, skinless chicken breast halves

1 1-oz. env. dry onion soup mix

1 10¾-oz. can cream of mushroom soup

2 C. sour cream

1 C. fresh mushrooms, sliced (optional)

Hot, cooked rice, noodles, or mashed potatoes

Ingredients

1 10¾-oz. can cream of chicken soup

1 C. chicken broth

1 1-oz. env. dry Ranch dressing mix

1½ lbs. boneless, skinless chicken breasts, cubed

1 8-oz. pkg. cream cheese

Hot, cooked rice

Ingredients

4 boneless, skinless chicken thighs, trimmed of fat and patted dry

½ C. chopped red pepper

3 garlic cloves, minced

½ C. Caesar dressing

Hot, cooked spinach fettuccine noodles

Ingredients

1½ lbs. bone-in chicken pieces, skin removed and patted dry

1 10¾-oz. can cream of mushroom soup

⅓ C. evaporated milk

1 pkg. stuffing mix with seasoning packet

1 ⅔ C. boiling water

CREAMY RANCH CHICKEN

1. Combine soup, broth, dressing mix, and chicken in slow-cooker.

2. Cover and cook on LOW for 3–4 hours.

3. Stir in cream cheese until smooth; serve over rice.

Makes 4 servings.

GARLIC CAESAR CHICKEN

1. Place chicken in slow-cooker. Cover with red pepper, garlic, and Caesar dressing.

2. Cover and cook on LOW for 4–6 hours.

3. Serve over spinach fettuccine noodles.

Makes 4 servings.

ONE-DISH CHICKEN SUPPER

1. Place chicken in slow-cooker. Combine soup and milk and pour over chicken.

2. Combine stuffing mix, seasoning packet, and boiling water. Spoon over chicken.

3. Cover and cook on LOW for 4–6 hours.

Makes 4 servings.

NO-DEFROST CHICKEN

1. Place frozen chicken in slow-cooker.

2. In a medium bowl, mix soup, mushrooms, salt, and pepper; pour over chicken.

3. Cover and cook on LOW for 6–8 hours.

4. Stir in sour cream; serve over rice or noodles.

Makes 6 servings.

Ingredients

6 frozen boneless, skinless chicken breast halves

2 10¾-oz. cans cream of chicken soup

1 4-oz. can sliced mushrooms

¾ tsp. salt

¼ tsp. pepper

½ C. sour cream

Hot, cooked rice or noodles

Ingredients

1 10¾-oz. can cream of chicken soup

¼ C. water

2 Tbsp. fresh lemon juice

¼ C. Dijon mustard

2–3 garlic cloves, minced

1 Tbsp. quick-cooking tapioca

6 boneless, skinless chicken thighs, trimmed of all fat

Hot, cooked rice or noodles

Ingredients

2–3 boneless, skinless chicken breast halves

2 C. chicken broth

2 garlic cloves, minced

1 Tbsp. Shirley J® Onion Seasoning

1 loaf frozen bread dough

½ C. freeze-dried mushrooms

¼–½ C. freeze-dried spinach

¼–½ C. freeze-dried red peppers

8 oz. cream cheese

DIJON CHICKEN

1. In a small bowl, mix soup, water, lemon juice, mustard, garlic, and tapioca.

2. Cut each thigh into 4 pieces and place in bottom of slow-cooker. Pour soup mixture over the top of the thighs.

3. Cover and cook on LOW for 3–5 hours.

4. Serve over rice or noodles.

Makes 4 servings.

SPINACH AND CHICKEN CALZONE

1. In slow-cooker, combine chicken, broth, garlic, and onion seasoning.

2. Cover and cook on LOW for 3–5 hours.

3. In the meantime, thaw bread dough.

4. Reconstitute freeze-dried mushrooms, spinach, and peppers.

5. Remove chicken from slow-cooker. Shred, using two forks.

6. Mix chicken with cream cheese and reconstituted vegetables.

7. Roll out dough into a long rectangle; cut into 4 even rectangles. Place ¼ of the chicken mixture down the center of each rectangle. Fold each rectangle over, then pinch the tops and sides of each to form a calzone. Bake at 350 for 15–20 minutes.

Makes 4 servings.

CHICKEN AND BROCCOLI TWISTED BREAD

1. Place chicken in slow-cooker. Top with broth, onion, and garlic.

2. Cover and cook on LOW for 3–5 hours.

3. In the meantime, thaw bread dough according to package directions.

4. Remove chicken from liquid and shred using two forks. Mix shredded chicken with cream cheese, broccoli, and red and green peppers. Set aside.

5. Roll bread dough into a long rectangle. Cut a 1½-inch strip of dough on each side, leaving dough connected at the top. Spread chicken mixture down the center of the dough. Fold sides of dough over into a braid and twist ends. Bake at 350 for 25 minutes or until bread is cooked through. Let cool for 10 minutes and then cut and serve.

Makes 6–8 servings.

Ingredients

3 boneless, skinless chicken breast halves

2 C. chicken broth

⅓ C. dehydrated onion

2 garlic cloves, minced

1 loaf frozen bread dough

1 8-oz. pkg. cream cheese

1 C. broccoli florets, blanched

1 red pepper, chopped

1 green pepper, chopped

HOME-STYLE CHICKEN AND STUFFING

1. In a bowl, combine soup, butter, ¼ C. water, stuffing mix, and seasoning packet.

2. Place chicken in bottom of slow-cooker and top with stuffing mixture.

3. Cover and cook on LOW for 4–6 hours.

Makes 4 servings.

Ingredients

1 10¾-oz. can cream of chicken soup

¼ C. butter, melted

¼ C. water

1 8-oz. pkg. cornbread stuffing mix with seasoning packet

4–8 chicken drumsticks, skin removed

Ingredients

2 lbs. boneless, skinless chicken
    thighs, trimmed of fat

½ C. soy sauce

⅓ C. packed brown sugar

2 Tbsp. sesame oil

3 garlic cloves, minced

Ingredients

1 10¾-oz. can cream of chicken soup

½ C. chicken broth

1 Tbsp. quick-cooking tapioca

1 lb. boneless, skinless chicken
    breasts, cut into 1-inch cubes

4 C. cooked rice

9½-oz. pkg. chow mein noodles

1 C. chopped celery

½ C. chopped green onion

1 20-oz. can pineapple chunks,
    drained

1 C. cheddar cheese, grated

½ C. almonds, slivered

3 medium tomatoes, diced

½ C. green pepper, chopped

ASIAN CHICKEN BARBECUE

1. Cut each chicken thigh into 4 pieces. Arrange chicken in the bottom of slow-cooker as flat as possible.

2. In a small bowl, combine soy sauce, brown sugar, oil, and garlic. Pour sauce over chicken.

3. Cover and cook on LOW for 2 hours. Turn chicken over and cook for 1 additional hour.

Makes 4 servings.

HAWAIIAN HAYSTACKS

1. Combine soup, broth, tapioca, and raw chicken chunks in slow-cooker.

2. Cover and cook on LOW for 3–4 hours.

3. On individual plates, serve chicken and gravy over rice. Top with remaining ingredients as desired.

Makes 8 servings.

Ingredients

2 lbs. boneless, skinless chicken thighs

¼ C. flour

½ tsp. pepper

½ C. soy sauce

⅓ C. brown sugar

3 garlic cloves, minced

1 Tbsp. fish sauce

1 Tbsp. rice wine vinegar

1 Tbsp. quick-cooking tapioca

⅛ tsp. ground red pepper

½ tsp. ground ginger or 1 tsp. fresh ginger, minced (optional)

2 Tbsp. sesame oil

Hot, cooked rice

ASIAN CHICKEN

1. Trim chicken of excess fat and cut each thigh into 4 large pieces.

2. Combine flour and pepper in resealable plastic bag. Drop chicken into bag and toss to coat.

3. In slow-cooker, combine soy sauce, brown sugar, garlic, fish sauce, vinegar, tapioca, red pepper, and ginger. Add chicken and stir to coat well.

4. Cover and cook on LOW for 3 hours. Stir in the sesame oil and cook for 1 additional hour.

5. Serve over rice.

Makes 4–6 servings.

CASHEW CHICKEN

1. Combine flour and pepper in resealable plastic bag. Add chicken and shake to coat with flour mixture.

2. Heat oil in skillet over medium-high heat. Brown chicken about 2 minutes on each side. Place chicken in slow-cooker.

3. In a small bowl, combine soy sauce, vinegar, ketchup, brown sugar, garlic, ginger, water chestnuts, and pepper flakes; pour over chicken.

4. Cover and cook on LOW for 3–4 hours.

5. Stir in cashews. Serve over rice.

Makes 4–6 servings

Ingredients

¼ C. all-purpose flour

½ tsp. black pepper

2 lbs. boneless, skinless chicken thigh tenders

1 Tbsp. canola oil

¼ C. soy sauce

2 Tbsp. rice wine vinegar

2 Tbsp. ketchup

1 Tbsp. brown sugar

1 garlic clove, minced

½ tsp. grated fresh ginger

1 4-oz. can water chestnuts

¼ tsp. red pepper flakes

½ C. cashews

Hot, cooked rice

SWEET AND SOUR CHICKEN

1. Place chicken in slow-cooker. Combine dressing, jam, and onion soup mix and then pour over the top of the chicken.

2. Cover and cook on LOW for 3–4 hours.

3. Break up chicken with two forks and coat with sauce. Serve over rice.

Makes 4 servings.

Ingredients

4 boneless, skinless chicken breast halves

1 C. Catalina or Russian dressing

1 C. apricot jam

1 1-oz. env. dry onion soup mix

Ingredients

1 small onion, finely diced

1 tsp. curry powder

1 garlic clove, minced

1 Tbsp. canola oil

4 boneless, skinless chicken breast halves, cut into ¾-inch pieces

1 C. coarsely chopped apple, divided

3 Tbsp. raisins

¼ tsp. ground ginger

⅓ C. water

1½ tsp. chicken bouillon granules

1½ tsp. all-purpose flour

¼ C. sour cream

½ tsp. cornstarch

Hot, cooked rice

CHICKEN CURRY

1. In a microwave-safe bowl, combine onion, curry powder, garlic, and oil. Cook on high for 4–5 minutes, stirring every minute, until onions are soft. Transfer contents to the slow-cooker.

2. Combine chicken, ¾ C. apple, raisins, and ginger in slow-cooker. In a small bowl, stir water into chicken bouillon granules and flour until smooth. Add to slow-cooker.

3. Cover and cook on LOW for 3–4 hours.

4. In a large bowl, combine sour cream and cornstarch. Drain all cooking liquid from the slow-cooker chicken mixture into the sour cream mixture. Stir to combine. Add sour cream mixture to the slow-cooker and stir well.

5. Cover slow-cooker and let stand 5–10 minutes or until sauce is heated through. Serve chicken curry over rice; garnish with remaining chopped apple.

Makes 4 servings.

Ingredients

cook's FAV.

2 garlic cloves, minced

⅔ C. chunky peanut butter

1 C. chicken broth

1 lb. boneless, skinless chicken breasts, cut into 1-inch cubes

1 C. shredded zucchini

⅓ C. soy sauce

1 tsp. sugar

12 oz. linguine or spaghetti, cooked

Peanuts and cilantro, for garnish

THAI PEANUT NOODLES

1. In the slow-cooker, combine garlic, peanut butter, broth, chicken, zucchini, soy sauce, and sugar.

2. Cover and cook on LOW for 3–4 hours.

3. Stir until smooth. Serve over hot, cooked fettuccine. Garnish with peanuts and cilantro.

Makes 4–6 servings.

ASIAN CHICKEN AND NOODLES

1. In a medium bowl, combine peanut butter, soy sauce, rice vinegar, lime juice, oil, chili sauce, ginger, salt, and garlic; whisk until smooth. Toss chicken into mixture and place in slow-cooker.

2. Cover and cook on LOW for 3–4 hours (watch to see that the peanut butter sauce doesn't start burning).

3. About 20 minutes before serving, cook 8 oz. linguine according to package directions. During the last 2 minutes of cooking, add carrots, snow peas, and bell pepper to the linguine. Reserve ⅓–½ C. of the cooking liquid; stir it into the slow-cooker mixture. Drain the pasta and vegetables and place in a large bowl. Pour the chicken mixture over the pasta. Toss well.

Makes 4 servings.

Ingredients

⅓ C. creamy peanut butter

¼ C. soy sauce

1 Tbsp. rice vinegar

1 Tbsp. lime juice

1½ tsp. oil

1 tsp. hot chili sauce with garlic

½ tsp. ground ginger

¼ tsp. salt

2 garlic cloves, minced

1 lb. boneless, skinless chicken breasts or thighs cut into bite-size pieces

8 oz. linguine

½ C. shredded carrot

¼ lb. snow peas, trimmed and halved crosswise

½ red bell pepper, cut into strips

TERIYAKI CHICKEN AND VEGETABLES

1. Place chicken in the bottom of slow-cooker. In a small bowl, combine broth, teriyaki sauce, onion, and garlic; pour into slow-cooker.

2. Cover and cook on LOW for 3–4 hours.

3. Add vegetables and turn slow-cooker to HIGH; cook for 10–20 minutes. Stir and serve over rice.

Makes 4 servings.

Ingredients

1½ lbs. boneless, skinless chicken thighs, cut into strips

½ C. chicken broth

½ C. teriyaki sauce

¼ C. dehydrated chopped onion

2 garlic cloves, minced

1 bag frozen broccoli stir-fry vegetables, thawed and drained

Hot, cooked rice

THAI CHICKEN AND NOODLES

1. Place chicken, bell pepper, broth, soy sauce, garlic, and red pepper flakes in slow-cooker.

2. Cover and cook on LOW for 3 hours.

3. In a small bowl, mix cornstarch with lime juice, stirring until smooth. Turn slow-cooker on HIGH. Stir cornstarch mixture and peanut butter into slow-cooker. Cover and cook 30 minutes or until sauce is thickened and chicken is no longer pink. Stir well.

4. Garnish with nuts and cilantro; serve over spaghetti noodles or rice.

Makes 4–6 servings.

cook's FAV.

Ingredients

1½ lb. boneless, skinless chicken breasts, cut into ½-inch pieces

1 red bell pepper, cut into short, thin strips

1 C. chicken broth

¼ C. soy sauce

3 garlic cloves, minced

¼–½ tsp. red pepper flakes (depending on taste)

2 Tbsp. cornstarch

¼ C. lime juice

⅓ C. chunky peanut butter

¾ C. chopped peanuts or cashews

¾ C. chopped cilantro

Hot, cooked spaghetti noodles or rice

Ingredients

2 cloves garlic, minced

⅔ C. peanut butter

1 C. chicken broth

1 lb. boneless, skinless chicken
   breasts, cut into 1-inch cubes

1 C. shredded zucchini

⅓ C. soy sauce

1 tsp. sugar

1 red pepper, cut into long, thin strips

1 Tbsp. lime juice

1 C. chopped cilantro, divided

12 oz. linguine or fettuccine noodles,
   cooked and drained

Chopped peanuts, for garnish

Ingredients

2 lbs. boneless, skinless chicken
   thighs, trimmed of fat, or bone-
   in thighs with skin removed

½ C. chicken broth

¼ C. peanut butter

¼ C. soy sauce

2 Tbsp. chopped fresh cilantro

2 Tbsp. lime juice

½ tsp. cayenne pepper

2 tsp. minced fresh gingerroot

¼ C. chopped peanuts

Chopped fresh cilantro

THAI PEANUT CHICKEN

1. In the slow-cooker, combine garlic, peanut butter, broth, chicken, zucchini, soy sauce, sugar, and red pepper.

2. Cover and cook on LOW for 3–5 hours.

3. Half an hour before you are going to serve, stir in lime juice and ½ C. cilantro.

4. Serve over noodles; garnish with remaining cilantro and peanuts.

Makes 4 servings.

THAI CHICKEN THIGHS

1. Place chicken thighs in slow-cooker. In a bowl, combine broth, peanut butter, soy sauce, cilantro, lime juice, cayenne pepper, and ginger. Mix well and pour sauce over chicken.

2. Cover and cook on LOW for 4–6 hours, until juices run clear when chicken is pierced with a fork.

3. Serve garnished with chopped peanuts and additional fresh cilantro.

Makes 4 servings.

THAI CHICKEN DRUMSTICKS

1. Place drumsticks in slow-cooker.

2. In a microwave-safe bowl, combine oil, 1 Tbsp. tomato paste, onions, and garlic; cook for 4–5 minutes, stirring every minute. Transfer contents to slow-cooker.

3. In a medium bowl, combine peanut butter, tomatoes, remaining tomato paste, soy sauce, salsa, ginger, and pepper. Stir to combine well; pour into slow-cooker.

4. Cover and cook on LOW for 4–6 hours.

5. Remove chicken from slow-cooker and roll each piece in the chopped peanuts. Arrange on broiler pan. Preheat broiler. Broil chicken 6 inches from heat source, turning frequently, until browned, about 6–8 minutes. Serve immediately.

Makes 12 servings.

Ingredients

4 lbs. chicken drumsticks, skin removed

1 tsp. canola oil

1 6-oz. can tomato paste, divided

2 onions, chopped

6 garlic cloves, minced

½ C. peanut butter

1 14-oz. can diced tomatoes, undrained

⅓ C. soy sauce

1 C. chunky salsa

¼ tsp. minced gingerroot

¼ tsp. black pepper

2 C. chopped peanuts

Ingredients

3 lbs. ground chicken

1 onion, chopped

6 garlic cloves, minced

¼ tsp. ground ginger

1 C. chicken broth

2 Tbsp. Worcestershire sauce

2 Tbsp. soy sauce

⅔ C. peanut butter

1 Tbsp. sugar

1 4-oz. can water chestnuts, drained

¼ tsp. pepper

3 Tbsp. cornstarch

⅓ C. lime juice

2 C. shredded carrots

1½ C. chopped peanuts

24–30 large lettuce leaves

ASIAN LETTUCE WRAPS

1. In a large skillet, cook chicken, stirring to break up meat. Drain chicken and place in slow-cooker.

2. Add onion, garlic, ginger, chicken broth, Worcestershire sauce, soy sauce, peanut butter, sugar, water chestnuts, and pepper; stir.

3. Cover and cook on LOW for 2–3 hours or until chicken is thoroughly cooked and mixture is hot and blended.

4. In a small bowl, combine cornstarch and lime juice; mix well. Stir into slow-cooker. Cover and cook on HIGH for 20–25 minutes or until mixture thickens.

5. To serve, set out filling from slow-cooker, shredded carrots, and peanuts; use lettuce leaves for wraps.

Makes 18 servings.

TURKEY LETTUCE WRAPS

1. In a skillet, brown the turkey. Season with the onion seasoning. Drain any grease and place in slow-cooker.

2. Add garlic, ginger, chicken bouillon mixture, Worcestershire sauce, soy sauce, peanut butter, sugar, and pepper to the slow-cooker. Stir.

3. Cover and cook on LOW for 4 hours.

4. Stir in lime juice and red peppers. Cover and cook on HIGH for 20–25 minutes.

5. To serve, set out filling, shredded carrots, and peanuts; use lettuce leaves for wraps.

Makes 6 servings.

Ingredients

1 lb. ground turkey

2 tsp. Shirley J® Onion Seasoning

2 garlic cloves, minced

1 tsp. freshly grated ginger

½ tsp. Shirley J® Chicken Bouillon dissolved in ⅓ C. hot water

1½ tsp. Worcestershire sauce

1½ tsp. soy sauce

3 Tbsp. peanut butter

1 tsp. sugar

Dash of pepper

1½ Tbsp. lime juice

¼ C. freeze-dried red peppers

½ C. chopped peanuts

½ C. shredded carrots

6 large lettuce leaves

GREEK CHICKEN AND RED POTATOES

1. Place potatoes and onion in the bottom of slow-cooker.

2. Place chicken on top of potatoes.

3. In a small bowl, combine the garlic, pepper, oregano, lemon pepper, salt, olive oil, and lemon juice. Spoon over the top of the chicken.

4. Cover and cook on LOW for 4–6 hours or until potatoes are tender.

5. Using two forks, shred the chicken.

Makes 5–6 servings.

Ingredients

2 lbs. small red potatoes

1 onion, quartered

2 lbs. boneless, skinless chicken thighs, trimmed of fat

4 cloves garlic, minced

½ tsp. pepper

1 Tbsp. dried oregano

1 tsp. lemon pepper

1 tsp. salt

1 Tbsp. olive oil

3 Tbsp. fresh lemon juice

Ingredients

6 boneless, skinless chicken thighs, trimmed

¼ C. flour

1 20-oz. can pineapple rings, juice reserved

¼ C. soy sauce

1 Tbsp. Worcestershire sauce

¼ C. brown sugar

1 Tbsp. lemon juice

1 tsp. garlic powder

1 Tbsp. quick-cooking tapioca

1 Tbsp. apple cider vinegar

1 green bell pepper, diced (optional)

Hot, cooked rice

Ingredients

1 medium onion, sliced

1 clove garlic, minced

1 lb. boneless, skinless chicken thighs, trimmed of fat

1½ tsp. lemon pepper

½ tsp. dried oregano

¼ tsp. ground allspice

4 pita pocket breads

½ C. plain yogurt

1 tomato, sliced

½ C. chopped cucumber

1 medium red bell pepper, sliced in thin strips

HAWAIIAN CHICKEN

1. Dredge the chicken thighs in the flour and place in the slow-cooker.

2. Combine ½ C. reserved pineapple juice, soy sauce, Worcestershire sauce, brown sugar, lemon juice, garlic powder, tapioca, and apple cider vinegar. Pour over the chicken.

3. Top the chicken and sauce with the pineapple rings.

4. Cover and cook on LOW for 4–6 hours. Add the green pepper if desired and cook uncovered on HIGH for an additional 30 minutes.

5. Serve over rice.

Makes 4 servings.

cook's FAV.

GREEK CHICKEN PITA FOLDS

1. In slow-cooker, combine onion, garlic, chicken, lemon pepper, oregano, and allspice; mix to coat chicken with seasoning.

2. Cover and cook on LOW for 4–6 hours.

3. Heat pita breads as directed on package. Meanwhile, remove chicken from slow-cooker; place on cutting board. Using two forks, shred chicken.

4. To serve, stir yogurt into onion mixture in slow-cooker. Spoon chicken onto warm pita bread. With slotted spoon, transfer onion mixture onto chicken; top with tomato, cucumber, and red pepper strips.

Makes 4 servings.

Ingredients

6 slices bacon, cut into ½-inch pieces

1 lb. chicken tenders, cut into ¾-inch pieces

1 medium onion, chopped

1 medium carrot, sliced

1 stalk of celery, diced

2 14-oz. cans chicken broth

1 10¾-oz. can cream of chicken soup

¼ tsp. dried marjoram

⅛ tsp. pepper

1¼ C. uncooked wild rice, rinsed and drained

Ingredients

1 carrot, grated

4 garlic cloves, minced

½ red bell pepper, sliced

½ C. chicken broth

3 Tbsp. soy sauce

2 boneless, skinless chicken breast halves, cut into long, thin pieces

½ tsp. garlic powder

2 C. fresh broccoli florets

HERBED CHICKEN AND WILD RICE CASSEROLE

1. In a skillet, cook bacon until crisp over medium heat. Stir in chicken and cook 3–5 minutes, stirring occasionally, until chicken is brown. Stir in onion, carrot, and celery; cook for 2 minutes, then drain.

2. Pour 1 can broth and cream of chicken soup into slow-cooker; whisk until smooth. Stir in remaining can of broth, marjoram, and pepper. Stir in chicken mixture and wild rice.

3. Cover and cook on HIGH for 30 minutes. Reduce heat to LOW and cook for 4–6 hours or until rice is tender and liquid is absorbed.

Makes 6 servings.

GARLIC CHICKEN AND VEGGIES

1. In slow-cooker, combine carrot, garlic, bell pepper, chicken broth, soy sauce, and chicken; stir to coat. Sprinkle with garlic powder.

2. Cover and cook on LOW for 3–4 hours, until chicken is tender and vegetables are cooked.

3. Blanch the broccoli florets; stir into the slow-cooker. Cover and cook on HIGH for 20 minutes.

Makes 2–3 servings.

GARLIC LIME CHICKEN

1. Place chicken in slow-cooker. Combine remaining ingredients and pour over chicken.

2. Cover and cook on LOW for 4–6 hours.

3. Serve chicken and sauce over rice.

Makes 5 servings.

Ingredients

5 bone-in chicken thighs, skin removed

½ C. soy sauce

¼ C. lime juice

1 Tbsp. Worcestershire sauce

2 garlic cloves, minced

½ tsp. dry mustard

½ tsp. ground pepper

Hot, cooked rice

ASIAN GARLIC CHICKEN

1. Pat chicken dry. Dredge in flour and place in bottom of slow-cooker.

2. In a small bowl, combine broth, soy sauce, lime juice, Worcestershire sauce, garlic, dry mustard, pepper, tomato paste, and tapioca. Whisk until smooth.

3. Pour sauce over the chicken and cover the slow-cooker.

4. Cook on LOW for 4–6 hours.

5. Garnish with cilantro and serve over rice. (If you'd rather shred the chicken or break it up into large chunks, use two forks to do so.)

Makes 4–6 servings.

Ingredients

1½ lbs. boneless, skinless chicken thighs or 2 lbs. bone-in chicken with skin removed

¼ C. flour

½ C. chicken broth

¼ C. soy sauce

2 Tbsp. fresh lime juice

1 Tbsp. Worcestershire sauce

4 garlic cloves, minced

½ tsp. dry mustard

½ tsp. ground pepper

1 Tbsp. tomato paste

1 Tbsp. quick-cooking tapioca

Cilantro and lime, for garnish

Hot, cooked rice

Ingredients

6 bone-in chicken thighs or
    drumsticks, skin removed

1 12-oz. bottle barbecue sauce

½ C. Italian salad dressing

¼ C. brown sugar

2 Tbsp. Worcestershire sauce

ZESTY BARBECUE CHICKEN

1. Place chicken in slow-cooker. In a bowl, combine barbecue sauce, Italian dressing, brown sugar, and Worcestershire sauce; mix well. Pour over chicken.

2. Cover and cook on LOW for 4–6 hours.

Makes 6 servings.

Ingredients

4 bone-in chicken thighs, skin
    removed and trimmed of fat

1 C. barbecue sauce

2 Tbsp. Worcestershire sauce

2 Tbsp. brown sugar

¼ C. Kraft® Balsamic Vinaigrette
    dressing

BARBECUE VINAIGRETTE CHICKEN

1. Place chicken in the bottom of the slow-cooker.

2. In a small bowl, combine remaining ingredients; pour over the chicken.

3. Cover and cook on LOW for 4–6 hours.

Makes 4 servings.

Ingredients

⅓ C. all-purpose flour

½ tsp. salt

½ tsp. pepper

2 lbs. chicken drumsticks, skin
    removed and patted dry

¾ C. chili sauce

½ C. grape jelly

CHILI SAUCE CHICKEN

1. In resealable bag, combine flour, salt, and pepper. Place chicken in bag and shake to coat. Place chicken in bottom of slow-cooker.

2. In a small bowl, combine chili sauce and jelly. Pour over chicken.

3. Cover and cook on LOW for 4–6 hours.

Makes 4 servings.

MANGO CHICKEN

1. Place chicken in slow-cooker and cover with salsa.

2. Cover and cook on LOW for 4–6 hours.

3. Using two forks, break up the chicken into large pieces. Stir in pineapple and cilantro and serve over rice.

Makes 4 servings.

Ingredients

2 boneless, skinless chicken thighs, trimmed of fat

2 frozen boneless, skinless chicken breasts

2 C. mango salsa

1 14-oz. can pineapple tidbits, drained

½ C. cilantro

Hot, cooked rice

KAYE'S CHICKEN

1. Dredge chicken in flour and place in bottom of slow-cooker.

2. In a small bowl, mix honey, soy sauce, tapioca, and lemon juice; pour over chicken.

3. Cover and cook on LOW for 4–6 hours.

4. Serve over hot, cooked rice.

Makes 4 servings.

Ingredients

4 bone-in chicken thighs or drums, skin removed and patted dry

¼ C. all-purpose flour

⅓ C. honey

¼ C. soy sauce

1 Tbsp. quick-cooking tapioca

⅓ C. lemon juice

Hot, cooked rice

Ingredients

1 tsp. canola oil

4 boneless, skinless chicken thighs, trimmed and cut into bite-size pieces

½ tsp. salt

1 Tbsp. fresh rosemary or 1 tsp. dried rosemary

1 ripe tomato, diced

1 small green bell pepper and 1 orange bell pepper, cut into long, thin slices

1 tsp. chicken bouillon granules

½ C. water

2 Tbsp. cornstarch

2 Tbsp. water

Hot, cooked rice

Ingredients

6–12 small red potatoes, quartered

1 tsp. dried oregano

½ tsp. salt

¼ tsp. pepper

6 bone-in chicken thighs, skin removed

¼ C. water

3 Tbsp. lemon juice

2 garlic cloves, minced

1 Tbsp. chicken bouillon granules

1 lemon

ROSEMARY CHICKEN AND PEPPERS

1. In a skillet, heat oil; place chicken in pan and sprinkle with salt and fresh rosemary (if using dried rosemary, add later). Brown the chicken for 3–4 minutes; place in slow-cooker.

2. Add tomatoes and peppers to chicken in slow-cooker.

3. In a small bowl, combine bouillon with ½ C. hot water until dissolved. Pour into slow-cooker.

4. Cover and cook on LOW for 3 hours, or until chicken is done.

5. Remove lid and sprinkle in dried rosemary (if not using fresh).

6. In a small bowl, stir cornstarch with 2 Tbsp. water until smooth; stir into the slow-cooker.

7. With the lid off, cook on HIGH for about 30 additional minutes until the rosemary is incorporated and the sauce is thickened. Serve over hot, cooked rice.

Makes 4 servings.

LEMON CHICKEN AND RED POTATOES

1. Place red potatoes in the bottom of slow-cooker.

2. In a small bowl, combine oregano, salt, and pepper; rub over chicken. Place chicken on top of red potatoes.

3. In a small bowl, mix water, lemon juice, garlic, and bouillon; pour over chicken.

4. Cover and cook on LOW for 4–6 hours or until potatoes are tender. Squeeze juice from fresh lemon over chicken before serving.

Makes 6 servings.

CHICKEN ALL DRESSED UP

1. In a small bowl, combine ketchup, brown sugar, lemon juice, mustard, and salt; stir well.

2. Place potatoes on bottom/sides of slow-cooker. Place chicken on top of potatoes. Pour ketchup sauce over chicken.

3. Cover and cook on LOW for 4–6 hours and serve.

Makes 4 servings.

Ingredients

1 C. ketchup

¼ C. brown sugar

2 Tbsp. lemon juice

1 Tbsp. mustard

1 tsp. salt

3 russet potatoes, halved

4–6 boneless, skinless chicken thighs

PINEAPPLE CHICKEN AND SWEET POTATOES

1. In a large bowl, combine ⅔ C. flour, salt, nutmeg, cinnamon, onion powder, and pepper. Coat chicken in flour mixture.

2. Place sweet potatoes on bottom of slow-cooker. Top with chicken.

3. In a medium bowl, combine soup, pineapple juice, mushrooms, 3 Tbsp. flour, brown sugar, and orange peel; stir well. Pour soup mixture into slow-cooker.

4. Cover and cook on LOW for 4–6 hours.

5. Serve chicken and sauce over rice.

Makes 6 servings.

Ingredients

⅔ C. flour

1 tsp. salt

1 tsp. ground nutmeg

½ tsp. ground cinnamon

⅛ tsp. onion powder

⅛ tsp. black pepper

6 boneless, skinless chicken breast halves

3 sweet potatoes, peeled and sliced into ¼-inch slices

1 10¾-oz. can cream of chicken soup

½ C. pineapple juice

¼ lb. mushrooms, sliced

3 Tbsp. flour

2 tsp. brown sugar

½ tsp. grated orange peel

Hot, cooked rice

PESTO CHICKEN

1. Cut each thigh into 4 pieces. Place chicken in bottom of slow-cooker.

2. In a small bowl, combine pesto, pepper, garlic powder, and tapioca; pour over the chicken.

3. Cover and cook on LOW for 3–5 hours.

4. Serve chicken and sauce over fettuccine.

Makes 4 servings.

Ingredients

4 boneless, skinless chicken thighs, trimmed of fat

½ C. prepared pesto sauce

¼ tsp. black pepper

½ tsp. garlic powder

1 Tbsp. tapioca

Hot, cooked fettuccine

SLOW-COOKED PULLED CHICKEN

1. Place chicken in slow-cooker. In a small bowl, mix tomato sauce, ketchup, brown sugar, cider vinegar, and garlic powder; pour over the chicken. Stir to coat the chicken well with the sauce.

2. Cover and cook on LOW for 4–6 hours, until chicken is fully cooked.

3. Remove the chicken from the slow-cooker and place it in a bowl. Using two forks, shred chicken. Return the shredded chicken to the slow-cooker and stir to mix well with the sauce.

4. Season with red pepper flakes, if desired.

5. Serve over toasted buns.

Makes 5 servings.

Ingredients

1½ lbs. boneless, skinless chicken breasts, halved

1 8-oz. can tomato sauce

½ C. ketchup

2½ Tbsp. brown sugar

2½ Tbsp. cider vinegar

2 tsp. garlic powder

Red pepper flakes to taste (optional)

Ingredients

6–8 boneless, skinless chicken thighs, trimmed of fat

½ C. all-purpose flour

1 1-oz. env. dry onion soup mix

1 16-oz. can jellied cranberries

1 C. Russian dressing

Hot, cooked rice

Ingredients

1 lb. boneless, skinless chicken thighs, trimmed of fat and cut into 1-inch cubes

3 C. chicken broth

¾ C. water

1½ C. uncooked long-grain brown rice

4 oz. smoked turkey sausage, diced

½ C. celery, thinly sliced

½ C. chopped onion

½ C. chopped green bell pepper

2 tsp. Cajun seasoning

2 garlic cloves, minced

⅛ tsp. hot pepper sauce, optional

1 bay leaf

1 14½-oz. can diced tomatoes, undrained

1 8-oz. can tomato sauce

CRANBERRY CHICKEN

1. Dredge the chicken in the flour and place in slow-cooker.

2. In a medium bowl, combine soup mix, cranberries, and Russian dressing; pour over the chicken.

3. Cover and cook on LOW for 4–6 hours.

4. Using two forks, break up the chicken into large chunks; stir well to coat with the sauce.

5. Serve chicken and sauce over rice.

Makes 6–8 servings.

CHICKEN JAMBALAYA

1. Combine all ingredients in slow-cooker; stir well.

2. Cover and cook on LOW for 4–6 hours, until rice is cooked.

Makes 6 servings.

TOMATO AND MUSHROOM CHICKEN

1. Cut each thigh into 4 pieces and place in slow-cooker.

2. In a medium bowl, combine the tomatoes, basil, garlic, soy sauce, mustard, mushrooms, and tapioca; stir to mix well. Pour over the chicken.

3. Cover and cook on LOW for 3–5 hours.

4. Serve over your favorite pasta.

Makes 5 servings.

Ingredients

2½ lb. boneless, skinless chicken thighs, trimmed of fat

2 C. diced Roma tomatoes

1 tsp. dried basil

2 Tbsp. minced garlic

2 Tbsp. soy sauce

1 Tbsp. dry mustard

1 6-oz. pkg. mushrooms, washed and sliced

1 Tbsp. quick-cooking tapioca

Hot, cooked pasta

UNCLE GARY'S ITALIAN CHICKEN

1. Arrange chicken in the bottom of slow-cooker. In a medium bowl, combine soup, tomato paste, onion salt, garlic salt, garlic, oregano, and mushrooms. Spoon sauce over chicken.

2. Cover and cook on LOW for 4–6 hours.

3. For last 30 minutes, sprinkle cheeses over top and let melt. Serve chicken and sauce over hot, cooked spaghetti.

Makes 4 servings.

cook's FAV.

Ingredients

1½ lbs. bone-in chicken pieces, skin removed

1 10-oz. can tomato soup

1 6-oz. can tomato paste

¼ tsp. onion salt

¼ tsp. garlic salt

2 garlic cloves, minced

¼ tsp. oregano

1 4-oz. can sliced mushrooms or ½ C. fresh sliced mushrooms

2 C. shredded mozzarella cheese (optional)

¼ C. Parmesan cheese

Hot, cooked spaghetti

Ingredients

4 boneless, skinless chicken thighs, trimmed of fat

2 8-oz. cans tomato sauce

½ C. Alfredo sauce

¼ C. Parmesan cheese

1 4-oz. can mushrooms, drained

1 tsp. Italian seasoning

1 large garlic clove, minced

1 Tbsp. quick-cooking tapioca

Salt and pepper to taste

Hot, cooked bowtie pasta

ALFREDO TOMATO CHICKEN

1. Cut each thigh into 4 pieces. Place chicken in bottom of slow-cooker.

2. In a medium bowl, mix the tomato sauce, Alfredo sauce, Parmesan cheese, mushrooms, Italian seasoning, garlic, and tapioca; pour over the top of the chicken.

3. Cover and cook on LOW for 3–5 hours.

4. Salt and pepper to taste; add more Italian seasoning to taste if desired.

5. Serve over bowtie pasta. Sprinkle with additional Parmesan cheese if desired.

Makes 4 servings.

Photography by Katie Dudley. www.katiedudleyphotography.com

SHIRLEY J® ITALIAN CHICKEN

1. Place the chicken thighs in the bottom of the slow-cooker. Sprinkle lightly with garlic salt.

2. In a skillet over medium-low heat, whisk the water and Shirley J® Whisk Bliss. Bring to a slow boil and simmer for about 7 minutes. Add the tomato sauce, tomato paste, seasoning mix, and mushrooms to the skillet. Stir. Pour over the chicken.

3. Cover and cook on LOW for 4–6 hours.

4. Serve over spaghetti and sprinkle with Parmesan cheese.

Makes 4 servings.

Ingredients

4 bone-in chicken thighs, trimmed, skin removed

Garlic salt

1 C. water

¼ C. Shirley J® Whisk Bliss

1 8-oz. can tomato sauce

1 6-oz. can tomato paste

1 Tbsp. Shirley J® Pizza and Pasta Seasoning Mix

1 4-oz. can mushrooms, drained

Hot, cooked spaghetti

Grated Parmesan cheese, for garnish

PARMESAN PEPPER CHICKEN

1. In a microwave-safe bowl, cook the onions and oil for 4–5 minutes, stirring every minute until onions are soft.

2. Place chicken in bottom of slow-cooker. In a medium bowl, combine cooked onions, bell pepper, mushrooms, and spaghetti sauce; pour over chicken and stir to coat.

3. Cover and cook on LOW for 3–5 hours.

4. Using two forks, shred chicken breasts. Serve chicken and sauce over angel hair pasta. Sprinkle with Parmesan cheese and salt and pepper to taste.

Makes 4 servings.

Ingredients

1½ C. chopped onions

1½ tsp. canola oil

1 lb. boneless, skinless chicken breasts

½ bell pepper, chopped

1 4-oz. can mushrooms

1 26-oz. can spaghetti sauce

4 C. angel hair pasta, cooked

½ C. Parmesan cheese

Salt and pepper to taste

Ingredients

6 boneless, skinless chicken breast
   halves

1 egg, beaten

1 tsp. salt

¼ tsp. pepper

1 C. dry bread crumbs

1–2 Tbsp. canola oil

1 16-oz. can pizza sauce

1 C. grated mozzarella cheese

Hot, cooked pasta

Ingredients

2 large chicken breasts

1 tsp. garlic salt

1 lime

1 egg

¼ tsp. pepper

1 C. dry bread crumbs

1 Tbsp. canola oil

1 26-oz. can pasta sauce

¾ C. mozzarella cheese

Hot, cooked pasta

CHICKEN PARMIGIANA

1. Dip chicken into beaten egg; sprinkle with salt and pepper. Roll in bread crumbs.

2. In a skillet, heat oil on medium heat; brown chicken on each side for about 2 minutes.

3. Place chicken in slow-cooker. Pour pizza sauce over the top. Sprinkle with cheese.

4. Cover and cook on LOW for 3–5 hours.

5. Serve chicken and sauce over pasta.

Makes 6 servings.

LIME CHICKEN PARMESAN

1. Cut the chicken breasts in half. Then cut them almost in half horizontally (butterflied). Open up the chicken and sprinkle the garlic salt evenly on each piece of chicken. Squeeze the juice of ¼ of the lime over the top of the garlic salt. Push each chicken piece back together.

2. In a small bowl, beat the egg and mix in the pepper. Carefully dip each piece of chicken in the egg, then roll in bread crumbs.

3. In a skillet, heat the oil. Brown the chicken for about 30 seconds on each side and place in slow-cooker.

4. Pour the pasta sauce over the chicken and then sprinkle the mozzarella cheese on the top.

5. Cover and cook on LOW for 3–5 hours.

6. Serve the chicken and sauce over pasta.

Makes 4 servings.

Ingredients

3 C. frozen primavera vegetable medley

1 14-oz. can artichoke quarters in water, drained

1 tsp. garlic salt

¾ tsp. ground black pepper

1½ tsp. Italian seasoning

6 chicken breasts, rinsed and patted dry

1 14-oz. jar pasta sauce

¼ C. chicken broth

1 tsp. crushed garlic

3 Tbsp. tomato paste

1 24-oz. tube pre-cooked polenta, sliced ½-inch thick

Grated Parmesan cheese, for garnish

CHICKEN WITH VEGETABLE RAGOUT AND POLENTA

1. In slow-cooker, combine frozen vegetable medley and artichokes.

2. In a small bowl, combine garlic salt, pepper, and Italian seasoning. Season both sides of the chicken breasts with mixture. Place chicken in slow-cooker on top of vegetables.

3. In a large bowl, combine pasta sauce, broth, garlic, and tomato paste. Pour over chicken and vegetables. Top with polenta slices.

4. Cover and cook on LOW for 3–5 hours.

5. Serve hot with grated Parmesan cheese.

Makes 6 servings.

CHICKEN TETRAZZINI

1. In slow-cooker, combine chicken, broth, apple juice, onion, salt, thyme, pepper, and parsley.

2. Cover and cook on LOW for 3–5 hours.

3. Turn to HIGH and add mushrooms to slow-cooker.

4. In a small bowl, dissolve cornstarch in water; stir into mixture in slow-cooker. Cover and cook on HIGH for 20 minutes.

5. Stir in spaghetti and half the Parmesan cheese. Cover and heat on HIGH for 5–10 minutes.

6. Spoon into serving dish; sprinkle with remaining cheese.

Makes 6 servings.

Ingredients

4 boneless, skinless chicken breast halves, cut into 2½-inch strips

1 C. chicken broth

½ C. apple juice

1 onion, finely chopped

½ tsp. salt

¼ tsp. dried thyme

¼ tsp. pepper

2 Tbsp. minced fresh parsley

1 4-oz. can mushrooms, drained

3 Tbsp. cornstarch

¼ C. water

8 oz. fettuccine, broken into 2-inch pieces, cooked, and drained

½ C. grated Parmesan cheese

ITALIANO CHICKEN

1. Wash chicken, pat dry, and season with garlic salt and pepper to taste. Place in slow-cooker.

2. Pour spaghetti sauce over chicken; sprinkle with cheeses.

3. Cover and cook on LOW for 4–6 hours.

4. Using two forks, break up the chicken; serve chicken and sauce over pasta.

Makes 6 servings.

Ingredients

6–8 boneless, skinless chicken thighs, trimmed of fat

Garlic salt to taste

Pepper to taste

1 26-oz. can spaghetti sauce

1 C. Monterey Jack/Colby blend cheese

3 Tbsp. Parmesan cheese

Hot, cooked pasta

Ingredients

1 lb. ground chicken

½ C. quick-cooking oats

1 tsp. chili powder

½ tsp. garlic salt

1 garlic clove, minced

1 egg

2 Tbsp. bread crumbs

CHICKEN MEATBALLS

1. In a medium bowl, combine all ingredients. Stir to mix well. Form into meatballs.

2. Place meatballs in the bottom of a large slow-cooker.

3. Cover and cook on HIGH for 2–3 hours.

Makes 4 servings.

Ingredients

2 Tbsp. canola oil

1½ lbs. chicken tenders, cut into pieces

1 14-oz. can diced tomatoes

1 8-oz. can tomato sauce

¼ C. dehydrated onion

1 4-oz. can sliced mushrooms, drained

2 garlic cloves, minced

¼ tsp. salt

½ tsp. dried oregano

¼ tsp. dried thyme

¼ tsp. black pepper

Hot, cooked spaghetti

CHICKEN CACCIATORE

1. In a skillet, heat oil over medium heat. Brown chicken on all sides and drain excess fat. Transfer chicken to slow-cooker.

2. Add tomatoes, tomato sauce, onion, mushrooms, garlic, salt, oregano, thyme, and pepper.

3. Cover and cook on LOW for 3 hours.

4. Salt and pepper to taste. Serve over spaghetti.

Makes 3–4 servings.

LOW-FAT CHICKEN CACCIATORE

1. In a microwave-safe bowl, cook the onions, 1 Tbsp. tomato paste, basil, and oregano for 4–5 minutes, stirring every minute until soft. Pour into the slow-cooker.

2. To the slow-cooker, add mushrooms, bell pepper, tomatoes, remaining tomato paste, tomato sauce, garlic powder, salt, and black pepper; stir to mix.

3. Cover and cook on LOW for 4–6 hours.

4. Sprinkle with salt and pepper to taste and serve over pasta.

Makes 4–5 servings.

Ingredients

½ medium onion, chopped

1 6-oz. can tomato paste

½ tsp. dried basil

½ tsp. dried oregano

½ lb. fresh mushrooms, halved

1 bell pepper, chopped

1 12-oz. can diced tomatoes

1 8-oz. can tomato sauce

½ tsp. garlic powder

½ tsp. salt

½ tsp. black pepper

2 lbs. boneless skinless chicken breasts, cubed

Salt and pepper to taste

Hot, cooked pasta

PORK DISHES

Choose pulled pork sandwiches or fall-off-the-bone ribs to satisfy the tastebuds of your family and friends. However you cook it, pork in the slow-cooker can't go wrong.

mustard

Rosemary

potato   saucy

BBQ

get together

savory   garlic   Ribs

pulled pork

pork chops

smothered

spicy

Ingredients

6 boneless or bone-in pork chops

¼ C. all-purpose flour

1 Tbsp. canola oil

1 C. Catalina or Russian dressing

1 1-oz. env. dry onion soup mix

1 C. apricot jam

Ingredients

4 slices bacon, cooked until crisp and crumbled

1 onion, diced

1 Tbsp. water

½ tsp. brown sugar

2 garlic cloves, minced

½ tsp. dried thyme

¼ C. flour

½ C. chicken broth

2 Tbsp. soy sauce

1 bay leaf

4 bone-in pork chops

Flour for dredging

Salt and pepper to taste

1½ tsp. cider vinegar

1 Tbsp. dried parsley flakes

APRICOT PORK CHOPS

1. Dredge pork chops in flour. In a skillet, heat oil; brown pork chops for about 2 minutes on each side.

2. Place pork chops in slow-cooker.

3. In a medium bowl, combine dressing, soup mix, and jam; pour over the pork chops.

3. Cover and cook on LOW for 4–6 hours.

Makes 6 servings.

SMOTHERED PORK CHOPS

1. Place cooked, crumbled bacon in bottom of slow-cooker.

2. In a microwave-safe bowl, cook the onion, water, brown sugar, garlic, and thyme for 3–4 minutes, stirring every minute, until onions are softened. Stir the flour, broth, and soy sauce into the onion mixture. Pour into the slow-cooker and add the bay leaf.

3. Dredge the pork chops in the flour; in a skillet, brown the chops for about 1 minute on each side. Season with salt and pepper to taste.

4. Nestle the pork chops into the sauce in the slow-cooker; cover and cook on LOW for 3–5 hours.

5. Transfer pork chops to a serving platter and tent loosely with foil.

6. Using a large spoon, remove the fat from the liquid in the slow-cooker. Discard bay leaf. Stir in the vinegar and parsley flakes.

7. Spoon sauce over the pork chops and serve.

Makes 4 servings.

APRICOT-GLAZED PORK CHOPS

1. Dredge the pork chops in a mixture of the flour, salt, and pepper.

2. In skillet over medium heat, heat oil; brown pork chops in oil for about 2 minutes on each side.

3. Place pork chops in slow-cooker. In a medium bowl, combine broth, apricot preserves, onion, and mustard; pour over pork.

4. Cover and cook on LOW for 4–6 hours or until tender.

5. Serve pork chops and sauce over rice.

Makes 8 servings.

Ingredients

4 lbs. boneless or bone-in pork chops

¼ C. flour

½ tsp. salt

½ tsp. pepper

1 Tbsp. canola oil

1 10¾-oz. can chicken broth

1 18-oz. jar apricot preserves

1 small onion, chopped

2 Tbsp. Dijon-style mustard

Hot, cooked rice

SAUCY PORK CHOPS

1. Season pork chops with salt, pepper, and garlic powder. In a skillet, brown chops on both sides in oil. Drain.

2. In a small bowl, combine ketchup, brown sugar, and liquid smoke. Dip browned pork chops in sauce mixture and place in slow-cooker.

3. Pour remaining sauce over pork chops.

4. Cover and cook on LOW for 4–6 hours.

Makes 4 servings.

Ingredients

4 bone-in or boneless pork chops

Salt and pepper to taste

1 tsp. garlic powder

1 Tbsp. oil

1¼ C. ketchup

½ C. brown sugar

1 Tbsp. hickory-flavored liquid smoke

Ingredients

4–6 bone-in pork chops

1 C. barbecue sauce

1 6-oz. can cola (don't use diet)

½ C. ketchup

2 minute prep

ALL DAY

COLA PORK CHOPS

1. Place pork chops in slow-cooker; pour barbecue sauce, cola, and ketchup over the top.

2. Cover and cook on LOW for 4–6 hours, or until tender.

Makes 4–6 servings.

Ingredients

4–6 bone-in or boneless pork chops

⅓ C. all-purpose flour

1 Tbsp. canola oil

1 C. Ken's® Creamy Balsamic Dressing

Salt and pepper to taste

CREAMY BALSAMIC PORK CHOPS

1. Dredge the pork chops in flour. In a skillet, heat the oil over medium heat; brown the pork chops on each side for 2 minutes.

2. Place pork chops in bottom of slow-cooker. Pour dressing over the top to cover the pork chops.

3. Cover and cook on LOW for 4–6 hours, until tender.

4. Salt and pepper to taste and serve.

Makes 4 servings.

Ingredients

2 boneless pork chops

¼ C. all-purpose flour

⅔ C. chunky tomato salsa, fresh or jarred

1 Tbsp. lime juice

1 Tbsp. orange juice

1 Tbsp. fresh grapefruit juice

CITRUS PORK CHOPS

1. Dredge the pork chops in flour.

2. In a skillet over medium heat, heat the oil; brown the pork chops on each side for 2 minutes. Place the pork chops in the slow-cooker.

2. In a small bowl, combine the salsa and juices; pour over the pork.

3. Cover and cook on LOW for 4–6 hours, until the meat is tender.

4. Serve immediately.

Makes 2 servings.

PORK CHOPS AND MUSTARD-SAUCED POTATOES

1. In large skillet, heat the oil; sauté the onion until soft and clear. Remove onions; set aside. Brown pork chops on both sides in hot oil. Remove from pan and drain on paper towels to absorb fat.

2. In a large bowl, combine soup, chicken broth, mustard, thyme, garlic, and pepper. Add potatoes and cooked onion, stirring to coat. Transfer to slow-cooker. Place browned chops on top of potatoes.

3. Cover and cook on LOW for 6–8 hours.

Makes 6 servings.

Ingredients

1 Tbsp. canola oil

1 medium onion, finely diced

6 pork loin chops, cut ¾-inch thick

1 10¾-oz. can cream of mushroom soup

¼ C. chicken broth

¼ C. Dijonmustard

1 tsp. dried thyme

1 garlic clove, minced

¼ tsp. pepper

6 medium potatoes, cut into ¼-inch slices

PORK CHOP DINNER

1. In a microwave-safe dish, cook onion and broth for 4–5 minutes, stirring every minute, until onion is soft. Add to slow-cooker.

2. In slow-cooker, combine soup, mushrooms, mustard, garlic, salt, basil, and pepper; add potatoes, stirring to coat. Place pork chops on top of potato mixture.

3. Cover and cook on LOW for 5–7 hours. Serve.

Makes 6 servings.

Ingredients

1 onion, diced

¼ C. chicken broth

1 10¾-oz. can cream of chicken soup

1 4-oz. can mushrooms, drained

¼ C. Dijon mustard

2 garlic cloves, minced

½ tsp. salt

½ tsp. dried basil

¼ tsp. black pepper

6 red potatoes, unpeeled, cut into thin slices

6 bone-in pork chops

PORK CHOPS AND SCALLOPED POTATOES

1. In a skillet, heat oil; brown pork chops for about 2 minutes on each side.

2. In a medium bowl, mix soup, sour cream, water, parsley, potatoes, salt, and pepper. Place mixture in bottom of slow-cooker.

3. Place pork chops on top of mixture; cover and cook on LOW for 4–6 hours.

Makes 4 servings.

Ingredients

1 Tbsp. canola oil

4 boneless pork chops

1 10¾-oz. can cream of mushroom soup

2 C. sour cream

⅓ C. water

2 Tbsp. fresh chopped parsley

6 C. thinly sliced potatoes

1 tsp. salt

½ tsp. pepper

Ingredients

6 medium red potatoes, quartered

6 pork chops, trimmed of fat

2 tsp. dried rosemary

¼ C. dried onions

1 celery stalk, sliced

1 10¾-oz. can cream of mushroom soup

1 tsp. Worcestershire sauce

1 4-oz. can mushrooms

Ingredients

6 pork steaks or pork chops

1 tsp. salt

¼ tsp. pepper

1 Tbsp. canola oil

¼ C. flour

Salt and pepper to taste

2 large onions, thinly sliced

1½ C. ketchup

1½ C. water

¼ C. vinegar

¼ C. Worcestershire sauce

2 tsp. salt

2 tsp. chili powder

2 tsp. paprika

1 tsp. pepper

ROSEMARY PORK CHOPS AND RED POTATOES

1. Place potatoes on bottom of slow-cooker.

2. Place pork chops on top of potatoes; sprinkle with rosemary, onion, and celery.

3. In a small bowl, mix soup, Worcestershire sauce, and mushrooms; pour over the pork chops.

4. Cover and cook on LOW for 4–6 hours.

Makes 6 servings.

BARBECUED PORK STEAKS

1. Season pork with 1 tsp. salt and ¼ tsp. pepper. Dredge in flour. In a skillet over medium-high heat, heat oil. Dredge pork chops in a combination of flour and salt and pepper to taste. Brown onions and pork in skillet, turning to brown both sides.

2. In a medium bowl, mix ketchup, water, vinegar, Worcestershire sauce, 2 tsp. salt, chili powder, paprika, and 1 tsp. pepper; pour over the pork.

3. Cover and cook on LOW for 4–6 hours.

Makes 6 servings.

SOUR CREAM PORK CHOPS

1. In a skillet over medium-high heat, heat oil. Combine flour, salt, and pepper; dredge pork chops in flour mixture. Brown in skillet, turning to brown both sides.

2. In slow-cooker, layer chops and onion slices. Pour chicken broth over layers.

3. Cover and cook on LOW for 4–6 hours.

4. In a small bowl, stir 2 Tbsp. flour into the sour cream until smooth. Stir sour cream into the slow-cooker and blend into the cooking juices. Turn slow-cooker to HIGH and cook for 15–30 minutes or until the liquid has thickened.

5. Serve the chops and sauce over rice, noodles, or mashed potatoes.

Makes 4–6 servings.

Ingredients

2 Tbsp. vegetable oil

½ C. flour for dredging

1 tsp. salt

1 tsp. pepper

4–6 boneless pork chops

1 onion, sliced

2 C. chicken broth

2 Tbsp. flour

8 oz. sour cream

Hot, cooked rice, noodles, or mashed potatoes

COUNTRY RIBS AND PEPPERS

1. Place ribs and sliced peppers in bottom of slow-cooker.

2. In a small bowl, combine the dressing, soy sauce, Worcestershire sauce, Parmesan cheese, and garlic powder; pour over the ribs.

3. Cover and cook on HIGH for 1 hour, then turn to LOW and cook for an additional 4–5 hours.

4. Let sit for 10 minutes; skim fat off the surface.

Makes 4 servings.

Ingredients

2 lbs. bone-in country-style ribs

½ medium green bell pepper, sliced

½ C. balsamic vinaigrette dressing

3 Tbsp. soy sauce

1 Tbsp. Worcestershire sauce

¼ C. Parmesan cheese

1 tsp. garlic powder

Ingredients

4 lbs. country-style pork ribs, cut into serving-size pieces

1 8-oz. can tomato sauce

½ C. cider vinegar

½ C. brown sugar

1 Tbsp. soy sauce

1 tsp. salt

1 tsp. chili powder

Dash cayenne pepper

BARBECUED SPARE RIBS

1. Place ribs in slow-cooker.

2. In a medium bowl, combine tomato sauce, vinegar, brown sugar, soy sauce, salt, chili powder, and cayenne pepper; pour over ribs.

3. Cover and cook on LOW for 6–8 hours.

4. Turn off slow-cooker and let sit for 10 minutes. Skim fat from juices before serving.

Makes 6–8 servings.

COLA RIBS

1. Place ribs in slow-cooker; sprinkle with onion soup mix. Pour cola over ribs.
2. Cover and cook on LOW for 6–8 hours.

Makes 4 servings.

Ingredients

2 lbs. bone-in country-style ribs

½ pkg. dry onion soup mix (0.5 oz.)

1 16-oz. can cola (do not use diet)

COUNTRY RIBS AND SAUERKRAUT

1. In slow-cooker, alternate layers of sauerkraut and ribs, starting and ending with sauerkraut.
2. Crumble bacon; mix gently into top layer of sauerkraut. Pour water over the top.
3. Cover and cook on LOW for 6–8 hours.

Makes 4 servings.

Ingredients

1 27-oz. can sauerkraut, drained and rinsed

2 lbs. country-style pork ribs, cut into serving-size pieces

6 slices bacon, browned

2 C. water

BBQ COUNTRY RIBS

1. In a small bowl, combine the vinegar, mustard, onion powder, salt, pepper, brown sugar, and barbecue sauce.
2. Place the pork ribs in the bottom of the slow-cooker.
3. Spoon the sauce over the top of the ribs; make sure ribs are coated well.
4. Cover and cook on LOW for 6–8 hours.

Makes 4–6 servings.

Ingredients

¼ C. red wine vinegar

2 tsp. ground mustard

2 tsp. onion powder

½ tsp. salt

¼ tsp. pepper

¼ C. brown sugar

8 oz. barbecue sauce

2 lbs. boneless country-style pork ribs

Ingredients

1 10¾-oz. can beef broth

3 Tbsp. honey mustard

¼ C. honey

½ C. water

¼ C. honey barbecue sauce

¼ C. soy sauce

¼ C. maple syrup

3 lbs. baby back pork ribs

HONEY RIBS

1. In slow-cooker, mix beef broth, honey mustard, honey, water, honey barbecue sauce, soy sauce, and maple syrup.

2. Slice ribs apart, leaving an even amount of meat on each side of the bone. Place ribs into the slow-cooker and make sure they are covered by the sauce. If there is not enough sauce, stir in a little additional water or beef broth to compensate.

3. Cover and cook on LOW for 6–8 hours, or until the meat falls easily from the bones.

Makes 6 servings.

Ingredients

½ C. ketchup

½ C. packed light brown sugar

½ C. cider vinegar

1 Tbsp. mustard powder

½ tsp. cayenne pepper

1 tsp. salt

½ tsp. pepper

2–4 lbs. boneless or bone-in country-
style pork ribs

ALL DAY

SWEET AND SOUR COUNTRY RIBS

1. In slow-cooker, combine ketchup, brown sugar, vinegar, mustard powder, cayenne pepper, salt, and pepper. Whisk to mix well. Add ribs to slow-cooker; toss with sauce.

2. Cover and cook on LOW for 6–8 hours, or until ribs are tender.

Makes 4–8 servings.

Ingredients

1 C. dried pinto beans

3½ C. water

¼ C. chopped onion

1 4-oz. can chopped green chilies

1 garlic clove, minced

1 Tbsp. chili powder

1½ tsp. salt

1½ tsp. ground cumin

½ tsp. dried oregano

1½-lb. boneless shoulder pork roast, trimmed of fat

1 10½-oz. pkg. corn chips

¼ C. sliced green onions

Optional toppings: shredded lettuce, shredded cheese, chopped fresh tomatoes, salsa, sour cream, guacamole

PINTO BEAN AND PORK CHALUPA

1. Soak beans in 8 C. water overnight. OR place beans and enough water to cover in a 3-quart saucepan; bring to a boil and boil for 2 minutes; remove from heat; let stand for 1 hour. Drain beans and discard liquid.

2. In a slow-cooker, combine 3½ C. water, onion, green chilies, garlic, chili powder, salt, cumin, and oregano. Add pork roast and prepared beans.

3. Cover and cook on HIGH for 2 hours. Reduce heat to LOW and cook for 6 additional hours or until pork is very tender.

4. Remove roast; using two forks, shred the meat.

5. Drain beans, reserving cooking liquid in a saucepan. Combine beans and meat; set aside. Skim and discard fat from cooking liquid; bring to a boil. Boil uncovered for 20 minutes or until reduced to 1½ C. Stir in meat and bean mixture; heat through.

6. Spoon meat mixture over corn chips; top with green onions and other toppings as desired.

Makes 6–8 servings.

PORK LOIN CHALUPA

1. Place pork, garlic, chili powder, green chilies, cumin, oregano, and salt in slow-cooker.

2. Cover and cook on LOW for 6–8 hours, until meat falls apart easily.

3. Using two forks, shred the meat. Add the beans; cook uncovered for 1 additional hour.

4. Spoon over tortilla chips; top with cheese, green onions, tomatoes, sour cream, and salsa as desired.

Makes 8–10 servings.

Ingredients

4-lb. pork loin roast

2 garlic cloves, minced

2 Tbsp. chili powder

1 4-oz. can green chilies

1 Tbsp. cumin

1 tsp. dried oregano

1 tsp. salt

1 14-oz. can black or pinto beans, drained

Tortilla chips

Toppings as desired: cheese, green onions, tomatoes, sour cream, and salsa

Ingredients

2 27-oz. cans Bavarian-style sauerkraut

2 lbs. Polish kielbasa sausage, pre-cooked and cut into 3-inch pieces

1 medium onion, thinly sliced

1 tsp. chicken bouillon granules

½ tsp. celery seed

Ingredients

1 lb. dried red beans

Water for soaking

Ham, cut into small chunks (as much as you desire)

1½ tsp. salt

1 tsp. pepper

4 C. water

1 6-oz. can tomato paste

1 8-oz. can tomato sauce

4 garlic cloves, minced

Hot, cooked rice

BAVARIAN DINNER

1. In bottom of the slow-cooker, layer 1 can sauerkraut, 1 lb. sausage pieces, half the onion slices, ½ tsp. bouillon, and ¼ tsp. celery seed. Repeat layers and cover.

2. Cook on LOW for 4–6 hours.

Makes 6 servings.

RED BEANS AND RICE

1. Soak beans in water for 8 hours. Drain and discard soaking water.

2. In slow-cooker, combine remaining ingredients except for rice; mix well.

3. Cover and cook on LOW for 6–8 hours, or until beans are soft.

4. Serve over rice.

Makes 8–10 servings.

PULLED-PORK-STUFFED BISCUITS

1. Place pork roast in slow-cooker. Fill slow-cooker with 1 inch water.

2. Cover and cook on LOW for 6–8 hours, or until meat is very tender.

3. Drain liquid. Using two forks, shred the meat. Pour barbecue sauce on the pork and mix.

4. Using a serrated knife, cut each biscuit in half. Put 1 Tbsp. pork on the center of each bottom biscuit. Cover each with the top of the biscuit; gather edges around the filling and press to seal.

5. Generously spray a 2-quart baking dish (that fits inside your large slow-cooker) with nonstick cooking spray. Arrange filled biscuits in a single layer in the baking dish, overlapping slightly if necessary. If all 8 biscuits don't fit in a single layer, spray a piece of foil on both sides with nonstick cooking spray. Place foil lightly on top of layer of biscuits and place the rest of the biscuits on top of the foil. When finished, cover the dish with another piece of buttered foil, buttered side down.

6. Place small rack in bottom of slow-cooker (if you don't have a rack, use crumpled balls of foil to keep the baking dish off the bottom of the slow-cooker). Add 1 inch of water (water should not come to top of rack). Place baking dish on rack.

7. Cover; cook on HIGH for 2 hours.

8. Meanwhile, prepare dipping sauce by combining vinegar, soy sauce, sugar, and oil in a small bowl. Stir until sugar dissolves.

9. Serve biscuits with dipping sauce.

Makes 8 servings.

Ingredients

1-lb. pork picnic roast

1 C. plain barbecue sauce

1 container large butter-flavored refrigerated biscuits (8 biscuits)

Dipping Sauce:

2 Tbsp. rice vinegar

2 Tbsp. soy sauce

1 Tbsp. sugar

1 tsp. sesame oil

Ingredients

1 large onion, sliced

2 2-lb. pork roasts

1 14-oz. can vegetable broth

1 12- to 18-oz. bottle barbecue sauce (use your favorite kind)

Coleslaw

BARBECUE PORK SANDWICHES

1. Place sliced onion in bottom of slow-cooker; place the pork roasts on top of the onion. Pour can of broth over the top.

2. Cover and cook on LOW for about 8 hours or until pork is very tender.

3. Using two forks, shred the pork. Pour barbecue sauce over the top.

4. Cover and cook on LOW for 2–3 additional hours until all flavors are blended.

5. Serve on a bun with coleslaw on top of the pork. (This makes a lot of sandwiches, so the recipe can easily be halved, or you can freeze the leftovers.)

Makes 10–15 servings.

Ingredients

1 4-lb. bone-in or boneless pork shoulder roast

Salt and pepper to taste

¼ C. water

Barbecue sauce (use your favorite kind)

Coleslaw

SHREDDED PORK SANDWICHES

1. Season pork liberally with salt and pepper. Place pork in the slow-cooker with water.

2. Cover and cook on HIGH for 1 hour. Turn to LOW and cook for 6–8 additional hours, until very tender.

3. Remove roast and discard fat and juices. Chop or shred the pork; return to slow-cooker. Mix a little barbecue sauce into the meat for flavor.

4. Cover and cook for about 1 additional hour, until meat is heated through.

5. Serve on warm split sandwich buns with coleslaw on top of meat.

Makes 10–15 servings.

Ingredients

3-lb. boneless pork loin roast

1 tsp. kosher salt

½ tsp. pepper

1 medium onion, sliced

6 garlic cloves, peeled

1 C. chicken broth

GARLIC PORK ROAST

1. Trim excess fat from pork. Rub the pork with salt and pepper.

2. Place onion and garlic in slow-cooker. Place pork on top of onion and garlic. Pour broth over pork.

3. Cover and cook on LOW for 6–8 hours or until pork is tender.

Makes 10 servings.

Ingredients

3–4 russet potatoes, peeled & cubed

8 cloves garlic, peeled

1 bay leaf

½ C. chicken broth

2-lb. picnic pork roast

1 tsp. kosher salt

2 tsp. canola oil

1 Tbsp. soy sauce

1 Tbsp. A1® Steak Sauce

1 Tbsp. lemon juice

SUNDAY PORK ROAST

1. Place potatoes, garlic cloves, and bay leaf in the bottom of slow-cooker. Pour broth over the top.

2. Rub the pork roast with the kosher salt. In a skillet, heat oil in skillet and brown the meat for 1 minute on each side.

3. Place the meat on top of the potatoes. Pour soy sauce, steak sauce, and lemon juice over the roast.

4. Cover and cook on LOW for 6–8 hours.

5. After meat is cooked, use the juices to make gravy, if desired.

Makes 4 servings.

SPICY CITRUS PORK ROAST

1. Place roast in slow-cooker.

2. In a small bowl, combine remaining ingredients until well blended. Spread mixture over tops and sides of roast.

3. Cover and cook on LOW for 5–7 hours.

4. Transfer to a cutting board and let stand 10 minutes before slicing. Serve with lemon slices on the side.

Makes 6–8 servings.

Ingredients

2- to 3-lb. pork butt roast

4 Tbsp. melted butter

Grated peel of 1 medium lemon

1 tsp. chili powder

¼ tsp. black pepper

⅛–¼ tsp. red pepper flakes

PORK ROAST AND POTATOES AND ONIONS

1. Make evenly spaced slits in roast; insert a sliver of garlic in each slit.

2. Place potatoes in slow-cooker. Add half of onion. Place roast on onions and potatoes. Cover with remaining onions.

3. In a small bowl, combine tomato sauce and soy sauce; pour over roast.

4. Cover and cook on LOW for 6–8 hours.

5. Remove roast and vegetables from liquid and place on a platter. Tent loosely with foil.

6. Combine cornstarch and water and add to liquid in slow-cooker. Turn to HIGH until thickened, about 20 minutes.

7. Serve over sliced meat and vegetables.

Makes 6–8 servings.

Ingredients

2½- to 3-lb. boneless pork loin roast

1 large garlic clove, slivered

5–6 potatoes, cubed

1 large onion, sliced

1 8-oz. can tomato sauce

1½ Tbsp. soy sauce

1 Tbsp. cornstarch

1 Tbsp. cold water

Ingredients

2-lb. pork roast

½ tsp. garlic salt

Pinch pepper

1 onion, sliced

1 6-oz. can root beer

¼ C. ketchup

2 Tbsp. tomato paste

1½ tsp. lemon juice

1 Tbsp. Worcestershire sauce

1 Tbsp. honey

1 Tbsp. quick-cooking tapioca

Ingredients

2-lb. picnic pork roast

Kosher salt

Chicken bouillon granules

Onion powder

1 C. water

¼ C. ketchup

2 Tbsp. mustard

1½ tsp. soy sauce

1½ tsp. Worcestershire sauce

½ tsp. garlic powder

1½ tsp. red wine vinegar

Salt and pepper to taste

ROOT BEER PORK ROAST

1. Sprinkle pork with garlic salt and pepper. Place onions in bottom of slow-cooker. Place pork on top of onions.

2. In a small bowl, combine remaining ingredients; stir with a wire whisk until blended. Pour over roast.

3. Cover and cook on LOW for 6–8 hours or until pork is tender.

4. Using two forks, shred pork.

5. Turn slow-cooker to HIGH and cook uncovered for 30–40 minutes to thicken.

6. Serve in tortillas or on toasted buns.

Makes 6 servings.

SHREDDED PORK SALAD

1. Place pork roast in slow-cooker. Season liberally with kosher salt, bouillon granules, and onion powder. Pour water into slow-cooker.

2. Cover and cook on LOW for 6–8 hours or until meat shreds easily.

3. Drain liquid from slow-cooker; using two forks, shred the meat.

4. In a small bowl, combine the ketchup, mustard, soy sauce, Worcestershire sauce, garlic powder, and red wine vinegar. Pour into the slow-cooker and stir to coat the meat. Salt and pepper to taste.

5. Serve pork over salad with your favorite toppings.

Makes 6–8 servings.

SLOW-COOKER PULLED-PORK TACOS

1. In a slow-cooker, combine the salsa, chili powder, oregano, cocoa, and salt. Add the pork and turn to coat.

2. Cover and cook on LOW for 6–8 hours. Meat should be very tender and should pull apart easily.

3. Using two forks, shred the pork and stir into the cooking liquid.

4. Serve with tortillas, cilantro, sour cream, lime, and extra salsa.

Makes 6 servings.

Ingredients

2 C. salsa, plus more for serving

2 Tbsp. chili powder

2 Tbsp. dried oregano

2 Tbsp. unsweetened cocoa powder

1 tsp. Kosher salt

2½-lb. boneless pork butt or shoulder roast, trimmed of fat

Corn or flour tortillas

½ C. fresh cilantro

¾ C. sour cream

1 lime, cut into wedges

Ingredients

¾ C. apple cider

1½ Tbsp. sugar

2 Tbsp. soy sauce

1 Tbsp. vinegar

1 tsp. ground ginger

¼ tsp. garlic powder

⅛ tsp. pepper

3-lb. boneless pork loin roast, halved

2½ Tbsp. cornstarch

3 Tbsp. cold water

Ingredients

6-lb. boneless pork roast

½ C. water

2 cans El Pato™ (Mexican-style tomato sauce)

1 C. brown sugar

4 8-oz. cans tomato sauce

TERIYAKI PORK ROAST

1. In slow-cooker, combine apple cider, sugar, soy sauce, vinegar, ginger, garlic powder, and pepper. Add roast; turn to coat.

2. Cover and cook on LOW for 6–8 hours.

3. Remove roast and keep warm.

4. In saucepan, stir cornstarch and cold water until smooth. Stir in juices from roast and bring to boil. Cook and stir for 2 minutes, or until thickened. Serve with roast.

Makes 8 servings.

CAFÉ RIO PORK

1. Place pork and water in slow-cooker.

2. Cover and cook on LOW for 6 hours, until meat falls apart.

3. Using two forks, shred pork; discard drippings.

4. Add the El Pato™, brown sugar, and tomato sauce; cover and cook on LOW for 2 additional hours.

5. Serve over salad, on tortillas, or in sandwiches.

Makes 15–18 servings.

ALL DAY

2 minute prep

ALL DAY

PASTA DISHES & SAUCES

Busy evening? No worries: Make dinner ahead of time in your slow-cooker. Serve your loved ones some cheesy and filling lasagna or tortellini and have everyone asking for "more, please!"

savory

noodles

Ravioli *fettuccini*

tortellini *creamy*

Cheeses penne

whole-wheat *garlic*

meatballs

basil Parmesan

Italian Lasagna

spaghetti sauce

Ingredients

1 lb. boneless, skinless chicken thighs

1 14½-oz. can diced tomatoes with juice

1 tsp. Italian seasoning

4 garlic cloves, minced

1½ tsp. sugar

⅛ tsp. crushed red pepper

2 C. frozen spinach

4 oz. cream cheese

1 Tbsp. tapioca

8 oz. penne or shell pasta, cooked

¼ C. toasted pine nuts

Salt and pepper to taste

Ingredients

½ lb. ground beef, browned and drained

½ lb. smoked sausage, sliced

1 16-oz. can marinara sauce

1 4-oz. can sliced mushrooms, drained

1 14-oz. can Italian-style tomatoes, undrained

9 oz. frozen cheese-filled tortellini

1 C. shredded mozzarella cheese

½ C. shredded cheddar cheese

THIEVES PASTA

1. Pat chicken dry and cut each thigh into 4 pieces.

2. In slow-cooker, combine chicken, tomatoes, Italian seasoning, garlic, sugar, and red pepper.

3. Cover and cook on LOW for 3–4 hours.

4. Place spinach in a strainer. Run hot water over it and drain as much water as possible. You may need to blot with a paper towel.

5. Add spinach, cream cheese, and tapioca to slow-cooker and stir.

6. Cover and cook for an additional 30 minutes on HIGH.

7. Add cooked and drained pasta and pine nuts; stir to combine. Salt and pepper to taste and serve.

Makes 4 servings.

CHEESY TORTELLINI

1. In slow-cooker, combine beef, sausage, marinara sauce, mushrooms, and tomatoes in slow-cooker.

2. Cover and cook on HIGH for 2 hours.

3. Add tortellini and cheeses and stir. Cover and cook on HIGH for an additional hour or until tortellini are cooked through.

Makes 6 servings.

THREE-CHEESE TOMATO MAC

1. Spray slow-cooker with nonstick cooking spray.

2. In a saucepan, combine diced tomatoes, milk, soup, water, ½ tsp. salt, ½ tsp. pepper, mustard, and paprika. Bring to a simmer; add the cheeses and whisk until melted. Stir in macaroni.

3. Pour mixture into slow-cooker.

4. Cover and cook on HIGH for 1½–2½ hours, until macaroni is tender.

5. Top with diced fresh tomatoes.

6. Salt and pepper to taste and serve.

Makes 6 servings.

Ingredients

1 14-oz. can diced tomatoes with juice

1 12-oz. can evaporated milk

1 10¾-oz. can condensed cheddar cheese soup

¼ C. water

½ tsp. salt

½ tsp. pepper

½ tsp. dry mustard

½ tsp. paprika

⅔ C. grated sharp cheddar cheese

⅔ C. grated Colby Jack cheese

⅔ C. grated mozzarella cheese

2 C. whole-wheat macaroni noodles, uncooked

Fresh tomato, diced

Salt and pepper to taste

Ingredients

½ lb. lean ground beef

½ lb. bulk Italian pork sausage

1 C. sliced fresh mushrooms

15–26 oz. marinara sauce (depending how saucy you like it)

1 14.5-oz. can diced tomatoes, undrained

9 oz. frozen cheese-filled tortellini

1 C. shredded mozzarella cheese

CHEESY ITALIAN TORTELLINI

1. Break beef and sausage into large pieces. In 10-inch skillet, cook over medium heat about 10 minutes, stirring occasionally, until browned. Drain grease.

2. Spray slow-cooker with nonstick cooking spray. In slow-cooker, combine meat mixture, mushrooms, marinara sauce, and tomatoes.

3. Cover and cook on LOW for 4–6 hours. About 30 minutes before serving, add tortellini to slow-cooker; stir gently to mix. Sprinkle with cheese. Cover and cook on HIGH an additional 15 minutes or until tortellini are tender.

Makes 6 servings.

MEATLOAF TORTELLINI

1. In a microwave-safe bowl, cook the onions, oil, garlic, and tomato paste for 3–4 minutes, stirring every minute, until the onions are tender.

2. Add the onion mixture to the slow-cooker; stir in the Alfredo sauce, tomatoes, tomato sauce, pepper, Italian seasoning, mushrooms, spinach, and meatloaf. Stir until combined; fold in the frozen tortellini.

3. Sprinkle mozzarella over the top.

4. Cover and cook on LOW for 3–4 hours.

Makes 4 servings.

Ingredients

½ C. minced onions

1 tsp. canola oil

2 garlic cloves, minced

1 Tbsp. tomato paste

½ C. Alfredo sauce

1 14½-oz. can diced tomatoes

1 8-oz. can tomato sauce

Pinch black pepper

1 tsp. Italian seasoning

1 C. sliced mushrooms

20 spinach leaves

½ lb. leftover meatloaf, crumbled

2 C. frozen tortellini

¼–½ C. grated mozzarella cheese

RAVIOLI CASSEROLE

1. In a skillet, brown chicken with garlic, onion powder, and garlic salt. Pour into slow-cooker.

2. Add remaining ingredients and stir to combine.

3. Cover and cook on LOW for 3–4 hours, or until noodles are cooked through.

Makes 4–6 servings.

Ingredients

1 lb. ground chicken

2 garlic cloves, minced

Pinch onion powder

Pinch garlic salt

8 oz. tomato sauce

1 14-oz. can diced tomatoes, undrained

¾ tsp. Italian seasoning

3 oz. frozen spinach, thawed and patted dry with paper towels

1½ C. whole-grain pasta shells, uncooked

¼ C. Parmesan cheese

½ C. mozzarella cheese

Ingredients

1½ lb. ground beef

1 medium onion, chopped

1 garlic clove, minced

2 8-oz. cans tomato sauce

1 14½-oz. can diced stewed tomatoes

1 tsp. dried oregano

1 tsp. Italian seasoning

Salt and pepper to taste

16 oz. bowtie pasta, cooked and drained

10 oz. frozen chopped spinach, thawed and drained

¾ C. shredded mozzarella cheese

½ C. grated Parmesan cheese

Ingredients

¼ C. minced onion

3 garlic cloves, minced

3 C. chopped fresh tomatoes or 2 14-oz. cans diced tomatoes with juice

1 6-oz. can tomato paste

1 tsp. salt

Dash of pepper

½ tsp. dried basil

½ green pepper, chopped

1 lb. bulk Italian sausage, browned and drained

1 4-oz. can sliced mushrooms

Hot, cooked spaghetti

ITALIAN BOWTIE SUPPER

1. In skillet, cook beef, onion, and garlic over medium heat until meat is no longer pink; drain. Transfer to slow-cooker.

2. Stir in the tomato sauce, tomatoes, and seasonings.

3. Cover and cook on LOW for 4–6 hours.

4. Increase heat to HIGH; stir in pasta, spinach, and cheeses. Cover and cook for 10 minutes or until heated through and the cheese is melted.

Makes 6 servings.

YUMMY SPAGHETTI SAUCE

1. Combine all ingredients except spaghetti in slow-cooker and stir to combine.

2. Cover and cook on LOW for 3 hours.

3. Salt and pepper to taste. Serve over spaghetti.

Makes 4–6 servings.

Ingredients

4 oz. cream cheese

½ C. sour cream

½ C. cottage cheese

8 oz. lean ground beef, browned and drained

1 26-oz. jar spaghetti sauce

6 oz. egg noodles, cooked and drained

Ingredients

1 Tbsp. olive oil

1 4-oz. can mushrooms

½ C. grated carrots

1 garlic clove, minced

1 lb. lean ground beef, browned and drained

2 14-oz. cans diced tomatoes

½ C. beef broth

1 6-oz. can tomato paste

1 tsp. salt

1 tsp. dried oregano leaves

½ tsp. dried basil leaves

¼ tsp. black pepper

1 Tbsp. quick-cooking tapioca

4 C. cooked spaghetti

Grated Parmesan cheese (optional)

MOCK LASAGNA

1. In a small bowl, mix softened cream cheese, sour cream, and cottage cheese.

2. In a separate medium bowl, mix beef and spaghetti sauce.

3. Put a little sauce in the bottom of the slow-cooker. Then layer noodles, cream cheese mixture, and meat sauce twice.

4. Cover and cook on HIGH for 2 hours.

5. Sprinkle with Parmesan cheese and serve.

Makes 4 servings.

ALL DAY

MAMA MIA SPAGHETTI SAUCE

1. Place all ingredients except for the spaghetti and Parmesan cheese in a slow-cooker.

2. Cover and cook on LOW for 6–8 hours or on HIGH for 3–4 hours.

3. Serve sauce over cooked spaghetti. Sprinkle with Parmesan cheese if desired.

Makes 5 servings.

CREAMY LEMON AND ARTICHOKE SAUCE

1. In the slow-cooker, combine Alfredo sauce, onion powder, artichokes, Parmesan cheese, and chicken.

2. Zest the lemon and add zest to mixture in slow-cooker. Juice the lemon and pour the juice into the slow-cooker.

3. Cover and cook on LOW for 3–5 hours.

4. For the last 30 minutes of cook time, take off cover and stir in mushrooms.

5. In a small bowl, stir cornstarch and water until smooth. Pour into the slow-cooker and stir into the sauce. Turn the slow-cooker to HIGH and cook uncovered for 30 minutes. When sauce is thick, serve over hot noodles; garnish with diced tomatoes.

Makes 4–6 servings.

Ingredients

1 26-oz. jar Alfredo sauce

1 tsp. onion powder

1 14-oz. can artichokes in water, drained and coarsely chopped

¼ C. Parmesan cheese

½ lb. boneless, skinless chicken thighs, cut into bite-size pieces

1 fresh lemon

1 C. fresh button mushrooms or 1 C. freeze-dried mushrooms

1 Tbsp. cornstarch

1 Tbsp. water

Hot, cooked spaghetti (or other pasta)

Diced tomatoes, for garnish

WHOLE-WHEAT LASAGNA

1. In a large skillet over medium-high heat, brown and drain sausage. Turn heat off and stir in red pepper, mushrooms, spaghetti sauce, tomatoes, and spinach.

2. In a medium bowl, stir egg into the cottage cheese; whisk to combine. Add cottage cheese mixture to skillet.

3. Using a ladle, spoon about ½ C. sauce into bottom of slow-cooker. Place 3 noodles on top, breaking them in half if needed. Continue to layer sauce and noodles, ending with a layer of sauce.

4. Sprinkle with mozzarella and Parmesan cheeses.

5. Cover and cook on LOW for 4–6 hours or on HIGH for 2–3 hours.

Makes 6 servings.

cook's FAV.

Ingredients

1 lb. Italian bulk sausage, browned and drained

1 red pepper, diced

1 C. diced mushrooms (optional)

1 26-oz. can spaghetti sauce

1 14-oz. can diced tomatoes

30 spinach leaves (can use more or less)

1 egg

1 16-oz. container cottage cheese

12 uncooked whole-wheat lasagna noodles

1 C. mozzarella cheese

⅓ C. Parmesan cheese

Ingredients

8 lasagna noodles, uncooked

1 lb. ground beef or bulk Italian sausage

1 tsp. Italian seasoning

1 28-oz. jar spaghetti sauce

⅓ C. water

1 4-oz. can sliced mushrooms

1 15-oz. container cottage cheese

2 C. shredded mozzarella cheese

Ingredients

2 large onions, coarsely chopped

2 green bell peppers, coarsely chopped

2 red bell peppers, coarsely chopped

5 garlic cloves, minced

1 tsp. dried oregano

1 tsp. ground cumin

1 Tbsp. quick-cooking tapioca

1 large tomato, cored and coarsely chopped or 1 14-oz. can diced tomatoes, drained

½ lb. ground turkey, browned and drained

½ lb. bulk Italian sausage, browned and drained

3 C. mixed cilantro leaves and stems

EASY LASAGNA

1. Break noodles in half; place half of noodles in bottom of greased slow-cooker.

2. In a skillet, brown ground beef; drain. Stir in Italian seasoning, spaghetti sauce, and water.

3. In slow-cooker, layer half of sauce, half of mushrooms, half of cottage cheese, and half of mozzarella cheese. Repeat layers.

4. Cover and cook on LOW for 3–5 hours.

Makes 6 servings.

GARLIC PEPPER SAUCE

1. In slow-cooker, combine all ingredients except cilantro.

2. Cover and cook on LOW for 5 hours.

3. Mix in cilantro.

4. Serve over pasta, rice, or spaghetti squash. If not using immediately, transfer sauce in 1-cup quantities to airtight containers. Freeze until ready to use, up to 3 months.

Makes 5 cups sauce.

CHICKEN AND SPINACH LASAGNA

1. In a medium bowl, combine chicken, pasta sauce, and undrained tomatoes.

2. In a separate bowl, combine the cottage cheese, cream cheese, egg, spinach, and Parmesan cheese until well mixed.

3. Spoon about ¼ C. of the tomato sauce in the bottom of the slow-cooker. Place 1½ noodles on top of the tomato sauce. Layer the cheese mixture, noodles, and tomato sauce 3 times.

4. Top with the grated mozzarella cheese.

5. Cover and cook on LOW for 3½ hours.

6. Let sit for 10 minutes and then serve. Dig down deep with serving spoon to get all the layers.

Makes 6 servings.

Ingredients

2 boneless, skinless chicken breasts, cooked and cubed

1 8-oz. can pasta sauce

1 14.5-oz. can Italian diced tomatoes

1 C. cottage cheese

4 oz. cream cheese

1 egg

1½ C. frozen spinach, thawed and drained of excess water

¼ C. Parmesan cheese

6 uncooked whole-wheat lasagna noodles (each broken in half)

½ C. grated mozzarella cheese

Ingredients

1 lb. bulk Italian sausage

½ medium onion, chopped

2 garlic cloves, minced

2 26-oz. jars tomato-based pasta sauce

¾ C. beef broth

8 oz. tomato sauce

2 tsp. Italian seasoning

2 25-oz. pkg. frozen ravioli (don't thaw)

2 C. shredded mozzarella cheese

½ C. Parmesan cheese, divided

Ingredients

12 oz. mild bulk Italian sausage

1 4-oz. can mushrooms

1 28-oz. can Italian crushed tomatoes

1 8-oz. can tomato sauce

1 6-oz. can tomato paste

⅔ C. water

1 medium onion, chopped

1 Tbsp. sugar

1 tsp. dried rosemary

¼ tsp. pepper

2 garlic cloves, minced

9–12 oz. fettuccine noodles

Parmesan cheese for garnish (optional)

YUMMY RAVIOLI

1. In skillet, combine meat, onion, and garlic. Cook until meat is browned; drain off grease. Stir in the pasta sauce, broth, and tomato sauce. Simmer for 3–5 minutes.

2. Pour 2 C. tomato sauce into slow-cooker. Add one package of frozen ravioli; sprinkle with half the mozzarella cheese and 2 Tbsp. Parmesan cheese. Add an additional 2 C. sauce, the other package of ravioli, the remaining mozzarella, and 2 Tbsp. Parmesan cheese. Cover with remaining tomato sauce.

3. Cover and cook on HIGH for 2½–3½ hours or on LOW for 5–6 hours.

4. Sprinkle with remaining Parmesan cheese, cover, and cook for an additional 10 minutes.

Makes 8–10 servings.

FETTUCCINE WITH SAUSAGE

1. In a large skillet, brown sausage; drain off fat.

2. In slow-cooker, combine mushrooms, tomatoes, tomato sauce, tomato paste, water, onion, sugar, rosemary, pepper, and garlic. Stir in sausage.

3. Cover and cook on LOW for 5–7 hours or on HIGH for 3–4 hours.

4. Just before serving, cook pasta according to package directions; drain. Serve sausage mixture over pasta. If desired, sprinkle with Parmesan cheese.

Makes 6–8 servings.

PENNE PASTA PIZZA

1. Spray slow-cooker with nonstick cooking spray and set aside.

2. In skillet, cook pork sausage until partially cooked, stirring to break up meat. Add onion and mushrooms; cook and stir until sausage is cooked. Drain thoroughly, then add spaghetti sauce and tomato soup and bring to a simmer.

3. Cook penne pasta for half of the time directed on the package; drain. In a large bowl, combine pasta, cream of mushroom soup, and cottage cheese; stir to blend.

4. In prepared slow-cooker, place half of pork mixture, half of pasta mixture, half of mozzarella cheese, half of cheddar cheese, and half of pepperoni. Repeat layers.

5. Cover and cook on LOW for 4 hours or until pasta is tender and casserole is bubbling.

6. Let cool for 15 minutes before serving.

Makes 8 servings.

Ingredients

1½ lb. pork bulk sausage

1 onion, chopped

2 4-oz. cans mushrooms, drained

1 26-oz. can spaghetti sauce (use your favorite)

1 10¾-oz. can condensed tomato soup

1 16-oz. pkg. penne pasta

1 10-oz. can golden cream of mushroom soup

1 C. cottage cheese

1 C. shredded mozzarella cheese

1 C. shredded cheddar cheese

1 4-oz. pkg. sliced pepperoni

PIZZA RIGATONI

1. In slow-cooker, layer half of each ingredient in order listed. Repeat.

2. Cover and cook on LOW for 4–5 hours.

Makes 6 servings.

Ingredients

1 28-oz. jar spaghetti sauce

12 oz. rigatoni, cooked and drained

1–1½ lb. ground beef or bulk Italian sausage, browned

3 C. shredded mozzarella cheese

½ lb. pepperoni slices

Sliced mushrooms (optional)

Sliced onions (optional)

STUFFED SHELLS

1. In a large pot, cook pasta according to package directions until just tender; drain.

2. In a skillet, brown beef or sausage, garlic, and onion; drain.

3. In a large bowl, combine beef mixture with cottage cheese, mozzarella cheese, Parmesan cheese, eggs, parsley flakes, and pepper.

4. Stuff cooked shells with beef mixture; set aside.

5. Pour half of sauce into slow-cooker. Arrange stuffed shells in sauce. Top with other half of sauce.

6. Cover and cook on LOW for 4–5 hours.

Makes 6 servings.

Ingredients

18 jumbo pasta shells

¾ lb. ground beef or bulk Italian sausage

1 garlic clove, minced

1 onion, chopped

1 C. cottage cheese or ricotta cheese

1½ C. mozzarella cheese

¼ C. Parmesan cheese

3 eggs

1 Tbsp. parsley flakes

⅛ tsp. black pepper

1 26-oz. can spaghetti sauce

PIZZA LASAGNA

1. Break 2 noodles to fit in bottom of greased slow-cooker.

2. In a skillet, brown Italian sausage; drain well. Stir in Italian seasoning.

3. Spread half the sausage mixture over the noodles in slow-cooker. Lay 6 pepperoni slices over sausage. Then layer a third of the spaghetti sauce, half the water, half the cottage cheese, and a third of the mozzarella cheese over meat. Add another layer of noodles, browned sausage, pepperoni, and a third of the spaghetti sauce. Spread remaining water and cottage cheese over sauce, then a third of the mozzarella cheese. Layer remaining noodles, sauce, and mozzarella cheese over top.

4. Cover and cook on LOW for 3–5 hours. Do not overcook.

Makes 4–6 servings.

Ingredients

6 lasagna noodles

6 oz. bulk Italian sausage

½ tsp. Italian seasoning

12 pepperoni slices

1 26-oz. jar spaghetti sauce

2 Tbsp. water

1 8-oz. container cottage cheese

1 C. grated mozzarella cheese

Ingredients

2 lb. uncooked boneless, skinless chicken breasts cut into bite-size pieces

1 26-oz. jar Alfredo sauce

1 26-oz. jar salsa

1 Tbsp. quick-cooking tapioca

1 13-oz. box penne pasta

Ingredients

1 lb. ground beef, cooked and drained

¼ tsp. garlic salt

2 8-oz. cans tomato sauce

Pepper to taste

1 C. sour cream

1 C. cottage cheese

8 oz. medium egg noodles, cooked and drained

Shredded cheddar cheese

TANGY CHICKEN PENNE

1. In slow-cooker, combine chicken, Alfredo sauce, salsa, and tapioca.

2. Cover and cook on LOW for 3–4 hours.

3. In a large saucepan, cook pasta until desired tenderness. Add pasta to slow-cooker and stir to coat.

4. Cover and heat until warmed through.

Makes 6–8 servings.

SOUR CREAM NOODLE BAKE

1. In a medium bowl, combine meat, garlic salt, tomato sauce, and pepper.

2. In a separate bowl, combine sour cream and cottage cheese in a separate bowl.

3. Layer half of noodles, sour cream mixture, and meat mixture in slow-cooker. Repeat.

4. Cover and cook on HIGH for 2 hours.

5. Sprinkle with cheddar cheese and serve.

Makes 6 servings.

CREAMY CHICKEN AND NOODLES

1. Cook noodles until barely tender and rinse.

2. In a large bowl, combine remaining ingredients and the noodles; make sure the noodles are separated and coated with liquid.

3. Pour into greased slow-cooker.

4. Cover and cook on LOW for 4–6 hours or on HIGH for 2–3 hours.

Makes 6 servings.

Ingredients

8 oz. egg noodles

3 C. chicken, cooked and cubed

½ C. celery, finely diced

½ C. onion, finely diced

1 4-oz. can mushrooms, drained

½ C. chicken broth

½ C. Parmesan cheese

1 C. sharp cheddar cheese, grated

½ tsp. basil

1½ C. cottage cheese

1 10¾-oz. can cream of mushroom soup

VEGGIE AND CHICKEN ALFREDO

1. In slow-cooker, combine chicken, onion, basil, olive oil, lemon pepper, and ginger; stir thoroughly.

2. Add broccoli, bell pepper, water chestnuts, carrots, and garlic; mix well.

3. Cover and cook on LOW for 4–6 hours or on HIGH for 2–3 hours.

4. Stir in Alfredo sauce, mushrooms, and cooked noodles.

5. Cover and cook on HIGH an additional 30 minutes or until heated through.

Makes 6 servings.

Ingredients

1½ lb. chicken breast, cut into ½-in. pieces

½ medium onion, chopped

1 Tbsp. dried basil leaves

1 Tbsp. olive oil

1 tsp. lemon pepper

¼ tsp. fresh ground ginger

½ lb. broccoli, coarsely chopped

1 red bell pepper, chopped

1 8-oz. can of sliced water chestnuts, drained

1 C. baby carrots

1 4-oz. can mushrooms, drained

3 garlic cloves, minced

1 16-oz. jar Alfredo sauce

8 oz. wide egg noodles, cooked and drained

Ingredients

6 lasagna noodles, uncooked

1 16-oz. jar Alfredo sauce

2 Tbsp. water

¾ C. chicken, cooked and diced

1 8-oz. container cottage cheese or ricotta cheese

1 C. grated mozzarella cheese

Ingredients

6 boneless, skinless chicken thighs, trimmed of fat

1 26-oz. jar Alfredo sauce

1 26-oz. jar marinara sauce

1 Tbsp. quick-cooking tapioca

1 Tbsp. Italian seasoning

1 14-oz. can artichoke hearts, drained and coarsely chopped

2 C. fresh mushrooms, sliced

12 oz. pasta, cooked and drained (use your favorite)

Parmesan cheese for garnish

CHICKEN ALFREDO LASAGNA

1. Break 2 noodles to fit into bottom of slow-cooker.

2. Layer a third of the Alfredo sauce, half the water, and half the chicken over the noodles. Spread half the cottage cheese and sprinkle a third the mozzarella cheese over the meat layer. Add another layer of noodles. Layer a third of the Alfredo sauce, the remaining chicken, the remaining water, and the remaining cottage cheese. Sprinkle with the second third of the mozzarella cheese. Layer the remaining noodles, sauce, and mozzarella cheese.

3. Cover and cook on LOW for 3–4 hours.

Makes 5 servings.

CHICKEN AND ARTICHOKE PASTA

1. Cut each thigh into 4 pieces. Place in slow-cooker.

2. Top chicken with Alfredo sauce, marinara sauce, tapioca, Italian seasoning, artichoke hearts, and mushrooms.

3. Cover and cook on LOW for 3–5 hours.

4. Stir in pasta until well coated.

5. Sprinkle with Parmesan cheese and serve.

Makes 6–8 servings.

CREAMY CHICKEN FETTUCCINE

1. Place the chicken in a slow-cooker; sprinkle with garlic powder, onion powder, and pepper. Top with soups.

2. Cover and cook on LOW for 3–4 hours. Stir in cheese and olives.

3. Cover and cook until cheese is melted.

4. Meanwhile, cook fettuccine according to package directions; drain. Serve with chicken and sauce.

Makes 6 servings.

Ingredients

2 lb. boneless, skinless chicken breasts, cut into cubes

½ tsp. garlic powder

½ tsp. onion powder

⅛ tsp. pepper

1 10¾-oz. can cream of chicken soup

1 10¾-oz. can cream of celery soup

4 oz. Velveeta® cheese, cubed

2 oz. sliced ripe olives, drained

16 oz. spinach fettuccine

Ingredients

5 boneless, skinless chicken breasts

1 tsp. salt

⅛ tsp. pepper

½ tsp. paprika

2 Tbsp. olive oil

1 onion, chopped

4 garlic cloves, minced

1 red bell pepper, chopped

1 26-oz. jar spaghetti sauce

½ C. water

1 tsp. dried Italian seasoning

1 4-oz. can mushrooms, drained

1 8-oz. pkg. cream cheese, softened

2 eggs

1 16-oz. container cottage cheese

2 C. frozen spinach, thawed and drained

½ C. grated Parmesan cheese

8 whole-wheat lasagna noodles

1 C. shredded mozzarella cheese

CHICKEN LASAGNA

1. Cut chicken breasts into 1-inch cubes. Sprinkle with salt, pepper, and paprika; toss to coat. In a large skillet over medium heat, heat olive oil. Add chicken; cook and stir until chicken is thoroughly cooked, about 9 minutes. Remove chicken from pan with slotted spoon. In drippings that remain in skillet, cook onion and garlic until tender. Stir in red bell pepper, spaghetti sauce, water, Italian seasoning, and mushrooms; bring to a simmer.

2. Meanwhile, in medium bowl combine cream cheese, eggs, and cottage cheese; beat until smooth. Stir in drained spinach and Parmesan cheese.

3. Break lasagna noodles in half.

4. Place about 1 C. chicken mixture in bottom of slow-cooker. Top with a layer of lasagna noodles, more chicken mixture, half the cream cheese mixture, and half the mozzarella cheese. Repeat layers, ending with cheese.

5. Cover and cook on LOW for 4–6 hours or until noodles are tender.

6. To serve, scoop down deeply into the slow-cooker to get all the layers.

Makes 10–12 servings.

CHICKEN AND BROCCOLI PASTA

1. In a microwave-safe bowl, combine the onion, garlic, 1½ tsp. oil, thyme, and red pepper flakes. Cook for 3–4 minutes, stirring every minute or so. Transfer mixture to the slow-cooker.

2. Stir in the broth, vinegar, and tapioca.

3. Salt and pepper the chicken; place in the slow-cooker.

4. Cover and cook on LOW for 4–6 hours.

5. Using two forks, break up chicken into large pieces.

6. Add the tomatoes, red pepper, Parmesan cheese, and cooked spaghetti; stir well.

7. In a microwave-safe dish, cook the broccoli with remaining 1½ tsp. oil for about 3–4 minutes, stirring every minute. Stir broccoli into the slow-cooker.

8. Cover and cook on LOW for 1 additional hour.

Makes 4 servings.

Ingredients

½ C. minced onion

3 garlic cloves, minced

1 Tbsp. olive oil, divided

½ tsp. dried thyme

¼ tsp. red pepper flakes

1 C. chicken broth

1 Tbsp. white wine vinegar

1 Tbsp. quick-cooking tapioca

Salt and pepper to taste

3 boneless, skinless chicken thighs, trimmed of fat

2 fresh tomatoes, diced

1 red bell pepper, diced (optional)

2 C. fresh broccoli florets

½ C. Parmesan cheese

6–8 oz. whole-wheat spaghetti, cooked

SIDES & SALADS

What can you bring to the potluck or the neighbor's party? Now you have an array of choices! Just pick one of your favorite sides, plug in your slow-cooker, and let it do the work. Your friends will be asking for the recipe and you'll be happy you didn't spend one more minute preparing food than you actually had to!

beans

scalloped

nuts yams

Squash

pot luck

creamy green beans

Au Gratin

fruit cheesy fresh

gathering Mexican rice

stuffing

taco salad

Ingredients

Desired number of potatoes

BAKED POTATOES

1. Prick potatoes with fork and wrap in foil.

2. Place in slow-cooker. Do not add water.

3. Cover and cook on HIGH for 3–4 hours or on LOW for 6–8 hours.

Ingredients

2 lb. russet potatoes, peeled and cubed

¾ C. balsamic vinaigrette salad dressing, divided

¼ C. Parmesan cheese

1 tsp. salt

¼ tsp. pepper

Salt and pepper to taste

BALSAMIC PARMESAN POTATOES

1. Place potatoes in bottom of slow-cooker. Pour ½ C. dressing over potatoes. Sprinkle with Parmesan cheese, 1 tsp. salt, and ¼ tsp. pepper. Stir until coated well.

2. Cover and cook on LOW for 6–8 hours.

3. Right before serving, pour additional ¼ C. dressing over potatoes and stir. Salt and pepper to taste.

Makes 4 servings.

Ingredients

2 lb. small red potatoes, quartered

1 8-oz. pkg. cream cheese, softened

1 10¾-oz. can cream of mushroom soup

1 1-oz. env. dry Ranch dressing mix

CREAMY RANCH POTATOES

1. Place potatoes in slow-cooker.

2. In a small bowl, beat cream cheese, soup, and Ranch dressing mix. Stir into potatoes.

3. Cover and cook on LOW for 4–6 hours, or until potatoes are tender.

Makes 4–6 servings.

CHEESY POTATOES

1. Combine potatoes, soup, cheese, sour cream, bacon, salt, and pepper in large slow-cooker. Stir to coat.

2. Cover and cook on LOW for 5–7 hours, until tender.

3. Top with extra cheese if desired and let melt. Serve.

Makes 8 servings.

8–12 russet potatoes, peeled and grated

2 10¾-oz. cans cream of chicken soup

1 C. grated cheddar cheese

2 C. sour cream

6 strips cooked bacon, cut into bite-size pieces

½ tsp. salt

½ tsp. pepper

Grated cheese (optional)

Ingredients

½ C. whole milk

1 10¾-oz. can condensed cheddar cheese soup

1 8-oz. pkg. cream cheese, softened

1 garlic clove, minced

¼ tsp. pepper

2 lb. russet potatoes, cut into ¼-inch slices

½ C. chopped onion

½ C. sharp cheddar cheese, grated, for garnish

Paprika, for garnish

POTATOES AU GRATIN

1. In a small saucepan, warm the milk over medium heat until nearly boiling. Remove from heat and add the soup, cream cheese, garlic, and pepper. Stir with a whisk until smooth.

2. Layer about ⅓ of the potato and onions in bottom of slow-cooker. Top with ⅓ of cheese mixture. Repeat layering until all ingredients are used.

3. Cover and cook on LOW for 6–7 hours, or until potatoes are tender.

4. Sprinkle with cheddar and paprika; serve.

Makes 6 servings.

Ingredients

4 C. potatoes, cooked, peeled, and diced

1 10¾-oz. can cream of chicken soup

1 C. sour cream

1 C. shredded cheddar cheese

¼ C. finely diced onions

½ tsp. garlic powder

½ tsp. pepper

POTLUCK POTATOES

1. Combine all ingredients in slow-cooker. Mix well.

2. Cover and cook on LOW for 2–4 hours.

3. Salt and pepper to taste.

Makes 6–8 servings.

GARLIC POTATOES

1. In a microwave-safe bowl, combine garlic, onions, and oil; cook 4–5 minutes, stirring every minute, until onions are soft.

2. Place potatoes in slow-cooker; top with onion mixture and garlic powder. Stir until potatoes are well coated.

3. Cover and cook on LOW for 4–6 hours, or until potatoes are soft but not turning brown.

4. Salt and pepper to taste.

Makes 6 servings.

Ingredients

6 garlic cloves, minced

1 medium onion

2 Tbsp. olive oil

6 russet potatoes, peeled and cubed

½ tsp. garlic powder

Salt and pepper to taste

PARMESAN POTATOES

1. Layer potatoes, onion, oregano, salt, pepper, and butter in slow-cooker.

2. Cover and cook on LOW for 3–5 hours.

3. Sprinkle with cheese and serve.

Makes 6 servings.

Ingredients

2 lb. red potatoes, cut into ½-inch wedges

¼ C. finely chopped yellow onion

1½ tsp. dried oregano

½ tsp. salt

Black pepper to taste

2 Tbsp. butter, cut into 4 pieces

¼ C. grated Parmesan cheese

Ingredients

1 C. dried pinto beans, rinsed and drained

4 C. water

PINTO BEANS

1. Soak beans in water overnight. Beans will expand, so make sure there is plenty of water. You can also use the quick-soak method: Place beans and enough water to cover in a 3-quart saucepan. Bring to a boil; boil for 2 minutes. Remove from heat; let stand for 1 hour. Drain beans and discard liquid.

2. Place beans and 4 C. water in slow-cooker.

3. Cover and cook on LOW for 4–6 hours until beans are soft.

4. Drain extra liquid and use as a salad topping or in recipes that call for a can of pinto beans.

Makes 8 servings.

Ingredients

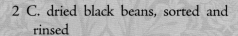

ALL DAY

2 C. dried black beans, sorted and rinsed

¾ C. chopped onion

1½ C. chopped bell pepper

5 garlic cloves, minced

2 bay leaves

1 14½-oz. can diced tomatoes, undrained

5 C. water

2 Tbsp. olive oil

4 tsp. cumin

1 tsp. salt

3 C. hot, cooked rice

BLACK BEANS AND RICE

1. Mix all ingredients except rice in slow-cooker.

2. Cover and cook on HIGH for 6–8 hours or until beans are tender and most of the liquid is absorbed.

3. Remove bay leaves.

4. Season with extra cumin and salt and pepper to taste. Serve beans over rice.

Makes 8 servings.

TOTALLY TASTY BLACK BEANS

1. Rinse beans and soak overnight in plenty of water. They will expand and become a bit soft.

2. Drain the beans; pour the beans into the slow-cooker. Fill the slow-cooker with water to 2–3 inches above the beans.

3. Stir in bouillon, dried onion, garlic, salt, and bay leaf.

4. Cover and cook on LOW for 8–10 hours or on HIGH for 4–5 hours.

5. Discard the garlic cloves and the bay leaf. Stir in red wine vinegar.

6. Serve using a slotted spoon.

Makes 6 servings.

Ingredients

1 C. dry black beans

1 Tbsp. Shirley J® Chicken Bouillon or 2 Tbsp. chicken bouillon granules

¼ C. dehydrated onion flakes

7 garlic cloves, peeled

1 tsp. salt

1 bay leaf

3 Tbsp. red wine vinegar

SEASONED BLACK BEANS

1. In a small skillet, sauté the onion in oil; add garlic and sauté. Stir in a little of the bean liquid and continue cooking until the onions and garlic are soft.

2. Pour the beans into the slow-cooker. Stir in the onion mixture and the spices. Cover and cook on LOW for 3 hours.

3. Just before serving, stir in the vinegar.

Makes 6 servings.

Ingredients

1 medium onion, chopped

1 Tbsp. oil

4 garlic cloves, minced

2 14-oz. cans black beans, drained, liquid reserved

1 tsp. cumin powder

1½ tsp. oregano

½ tsp. salt

1 Tbsp. red wine vinegar

Ingredients

½ C. diced onions

3 garlic cloves, minced

1 Tbsp. oil

2½ C. chicken broth

1 bay leaf

¼ tsp. pepper

1 C. wild rice, uncooked

1 C. fresh mushrooms, sliced

WILD RICE

1. In a microwave-safe dish, cook the onions, garlic, and oil for 4–5 minutes, stirring every minute, until onions are soft. Transfer to slow-cooker.

2. In a saucepan over medium-high heat, bring broth to a boil. Pour broth, bay leaf, pepper, rice, and mushrooms into slow-cooker.

3. Cover and cook on HIGH for 2½–3 hours, or until rice is soft and liquid is absorbed.

Makes 4 servings.

SPAGHETTI SQUASH

1. Using a fork, poke holes in the squash.

2. Put the squash in the slow-cooker; pour water over squash.

3. Cover and cook on LOW for 4–6 hours.

4. Cut the squash in half and scoop out seeds. Use a fork to scoop out the spaghetti-like strands of squash. Serve with your favorite sauce.

Makes 6–8 servings.

2 minute prep

Ingredients

Spaghetti squash (do not cut)

2 C. water

BANANA SQUASH

1. Place slices of squash, skin side down, in bottom of slow-cooker.

2. Cook on LOW for 3–5 hours.

3. Serve with butter, brown sugar, salt, and pepper.

Makes 6 servings.

Ingredients

Banana squash, seeded and cut in slices

Butter

Brown sugar

Salt and pepper to taste

SQUASH CASSEROLE

1. In a medium bowl, combine squash, onion, carrot, and soup.

2. In a separate bowl, combine sour cream and flour. Stir sour cream mixture into squash.

3. In a medium bowl, toss stuffing mix with butter. Spread half of stuffing mix in bottom of slow-cooker.

4. Spread vegetable mixture on top. Top with remaining stuffing mix.

5. Cover and cook on LOW for 4–6 hours.

Makes 4–6 servings.

Ingredients

2 lb. yellow summer squash or zucchini, thinly sliced (about 6 C.)

½ medium onion, finely diced

1 C. shredded carrot

1 10¾-oz. can cream of chicken soup

1 C. sour cream

¼ C. flour

1 8-oz. pkg. stuffing mix

½ C. butter or margarine, melted

Ingredients

6 yams

5 cooking apples

1 C. sugar

2 C. water

5 Tbsp. cornstarch

½ C. butter (no substitutes)

CANDIED YAMS

1. Peel yams and cut into thick slices.

2. Peel, core, and slice apples.

3. Layer yams and apple slices in slow-cooker, alternating layers.

4. In a saucepan, combine sugar, water, cornstarch, and butter. Cook and stir until thick and clear.

5. Pour sauce over apples and yams.

6. Cover and cook on LOW for 3–5 hours, or until yams are tender.

Makes 10 servings.

Ingredients

2–3 yams, sliced into ½-inch disks

¼ C. butter, melted

¼ C. brown sugar

1 tsp. salt

½ tsp. pepper

YAMMY YAMS

1. Place sliced yams into slow-cooker.

2. In a small bowl, combine the butter and brown sugar; stir. Pour over the top of yams and stir to coat. Sprinkle salt and pepper over the top and stir.

3. Cover and cook on LOW for 3–4 hours.

Makes 4–6 servings.

SWEET POTATOES

1. Using a fork, poke holes in desired number of sweet potatoes (peeled or unpeeled). Wrap in foil and place in slow-cooker.

2. Cover and cook on LOW for 3–4 hours.

3. Serve with butter, salt, and pepper, or mash and use as a baby food.

MASHED SWEET POTATOES

1. Place potatoes, water, and salt in slow-cooker.

2. Cover and cook on LOW for about 4–6 hours.

3. Drain the potatoes and return them to the slow-cooker.

4. Using a fork or potato masher, mash the potatoes. Stir in the butter (until melted) and milk.

5. Salt and pepper to taste and serve.

Makes 6–8 servings.

Ingredients

4 medium sweet potatoes, peeled and sliced ¼ inch thick

1½ C. water

1 tsp. salt

2 Tbsp. butter

2 Tbsp. milk

Salt and pepper to taste

MASHED POTATOES WITH SKINS

1. Cut up potatoes into little cubes. Place in slow-cooker along with the garlic salt. Stir to coat.

2. Cover and cook on LOW for 5–7 hours, or until very soft.

3. Using a hand mixer, cream the potatoes and the cream cheese. Blend in milk, sour cream, and salt and pepper to taste.

4. Serve with or without gravy.

Makes 5–7 servings.

Ingredients

5 medium russet potatoes (do not peel)

1 tsp. garlic salt

2 oz. cream cheese, softened

¼ C. milk

¼ C. sour cream

Salt and pepper to taste

BUTTERMILK MASHED POTATOES

1. Place potatoes, water, garlic, bay leaf, and 1 tsp. salt in slow-cooker.

2. Cover and cook on LOW for 4–6 hours, or until potatoes are tender.

3. Drain potatoes and discard the bay leaf and garlic cloves.

4. Using a potato masher or fork, mash the potatoes. Stir in the butter and buttermilk.

5. Stir in the chives and salt and pepper to taste. Serve.

Makes 8 servings.

Ingredients

3 lb. russet potatoes (about 6 medium), peeled and cubed

1½ C. water

2 garlic cloves, peeled

1 bay leaf

1 tsp. salt

3 Tbsp. butter

½ C. warmed buttermilk

2 Tbsp. fresh or freeze-dried chives

Salt and pepper to taste

EDIBLE COOKED CARROTS

1. Place carrots, water, sugar, and ½ tsp. salt in slow-cooker.

2. Cover and cook on LOW for 4–6 hours.

3. Drain water and return carrots to slow-cooker. Stir in garlic powder, parsley flakes, lemon pepper, and butter.

4. Salt and pepper to taste and serve.

Makes 6 servings.

Ingredients

1 lb. carrots, peeled and sliced about ¼ inch thick

½ C. water

1 tsp. sugar

½ tsp. salt

¼ tsp. garlic powder

1 tsp. parsley flakes

1 tsp. lemon pepper

1 Tbsp. butter

Salt and pepper to taste

Ingredients

3 C. finely chopped celery

½ C. finely chopped onion

1½ tsp. dried sage

1 tsp. salt

½ tsp. pepper

1½ C. chicken broth

¼ tsp. parsley

¼ tsp. rosemary

¼ tsp. thyme

14–15 C. stale bread cubes

¼ C. melted butter

Ingredients

1 medium onion, diced

1 Tbsp. canola oil

1 medium to large zucchini, peeled and sliced

1 14-oz. can diced tomatoes

¼ tsp. salt

1 tsp. dried basil

8 oz. cheddar cheese, shredded

THANKSGIVING STUFFING

1. In microwave-safe bowl, combine the celery, onion, sage, salt, pepper, broth, parsley, rosemary, and thyme. Cook for 5 minutes, stirring every minute. Transfer to slow-cooker.

2. Stir the bread cubes into the slow-cooker and mix well. Toss with melted butter.

3. Cover and cook on LOW for 4–5 hours. Remove lid and turn to HIGH. Cook for 1 additional hour without the lid.

Makes 10–12 servings.

ZUCCHINI SPECIAL

1. In a microwave-safe dish, cook the onion and oil for 4–5 minutes, stirring every minute, until onions are soft.

2. Layer zucchini, onion, and tomatoes in slow-cooker. Sprinkle with salt, basil, and cheese.

3. Cover and cook on LOW for 3–5 hours.

Makes 4 servings.

ALFREDO GREEN BEAN CASSEROLE

1. Spray slow-cooker with nonstick cooking spray.

2. In large bowl, mix beans, water chestnuts, salt, and Alfredo sauce. Fold in half of the French-fried onions. Spoon mixture into slow-cooker.

3. Cover and cook on LOW for 3–4 hours, stirring after 1–1½ hours.

4. Just before serving, heat remaining half of onions in a 6-inch skillet over medium-high heat for 2–3 minutes, stirring frequently, until hot.

5. Stir bean mixture; sprinkle with heated onions and serve.

Makes 10 servings.

Ingredients

2 1-lb. bags frozen cut green beans

1 8-oz. can sliced water chestnuts, drained

¼ tsp. salt

1 10-oz. jar refrigerated Alfredo pasta sauce

1 2.8-oz. can French-fried onions

CAULIFLOWER MASHED POTATOES

1. Cut up cauliflower into florets. Place in slow-cooker. Cover entirely with water.

2. Cover and cook on LOW for 4–6 hours, or until cauliflower is very soft. Drain water.

3. Using a hand mixer, cream the cauliflower into a smooth, creamy, mashed potato-like texture.

4. Season with butter, salt, and pepper to taste. Serve in the place of mashed potatoes.

Makes 4–6 servings.

Ingredients

1 head cauliflower

Water

Butter

Salt and pepper to taste

Ingredients

1 2-lb. bag frozen corn kernels

2 Tbsp. butter, cubed

1 large green bell pepper, finely chopped

1 tsp. salt

½ tsp. ground cumin

¼ tsp. black pepper

3 oz. cream cheese, cubed

1 C. shredded sharp cheddar cheese

CHEESY CORN AND PEPPERS

1. Coat slow-cooker with nonstick cooking spray. In slow-cooker, combine corn, butter, bell pepper, salt, cumin, and black pepper; stir.

2. Cover and cook on HIGH for 2 hours.

3. Add cheeses, stir to blend. Cover and cook 15 additional minutes or until cheeses melt.

Makes 8 servings.

Ingredients

1 2-lb. bag frozen mixed veggies

2 Tbsp. butter, cubed

1 medium red bell pepper, diced

1 tsp. salt

½ tsp. cumin

¼ tsp. black pepper

3 oz. cream cheese, cubed

1 C. shredded sharp cheddar cheese

MIXED VEGGIES CON QUESO

1. Combine veggies, butter, red pepper, salt, cumin, and black pepper in slow-cooker; stir.

2. Cover and cook on HIGH for 2 hours.

3. Add cheeses; stir to blend. Cover and cook for 15 additional minutes or until cheese melts.

Makes 8 servings.

BARLEY WITH PINE NUTS

1. In a small skillet, melt butter; add onion. Cook and stir until onion is lightly browned, about 2 minutes. Transfer to a small slow-cooker.

2. Add barley, broth, salt, and pepper. Stir in raisins.

3. Cover and cook on LOW for 3 hours.

4. Stir in pine nuts and serve immediately.

Makes 4 servings.

CORN ON THE COB

1. Place desired number of husked corn cobs in slow-cooker. Cover with water.

2. Cover and cook on LOW for 2 hours.

Ingredients

Corn on the cob

FRUIT, NUT, AND WHEAT BERRY SALAD

1. Finely grate the zest from the orange into a large serving bowl. Juice the orange into a small separate bowl and toss in the cranberries. Let the mixture sit at room temperature for 20 minutes.

2. Mix the wheat berries, diced apple, and nuts with the orange zest. Drain the cranberries, reserving the juice, and toss the cranberries into the wheat berry mixture.

3. Mix the reserved orange juice, vinegar, oil, honey, salt, and pepper. Pour over the salad and mix well. Cover and refrigerate for at least an hour to blend flavors.

Makes 6–8 servings.

Basic Cooked Wheat Berries:

⅔ C. wheat, 4 C. water, 1 tsp. salt

1. Place wheat, water, and salt in 4- to 6-quart slow-cooker.

2. Cover and cook on HIGH for 3–4 hours or on LOW for 6–8 hours, or until the wheat is chewy.

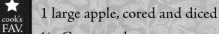

Ingredients

1 orange

⅓ C. dried cranberries

2 C. cooked wheat berries (see recipe at left)

1 large apple, cored and diced

½ C. toasted pecans or walnuts, coarsely chopped

Dressing:

Reserved orange juice

3 Tbsp. vinegar

3 Tbsp. vegetable oil

1 Tbsp. honey

¼ tsp. salt

¼ tsp. black pepper

GARLIC CAESAR CHICKEN SALAD

1. Place chicken in slow-cooker. In a small bowl, mix dressing, lime juice, garlic powder, and paprika; spoon over chicken.

2. Cover and cook on LOW for 2–4 hours.

3. Serve over the top of crisp romaine lettuce. Add cheese, tomatoes, and other veggies of your choice.

Makes 2 servings.

Ingredients

½ lb. chicken tenders

¼ C. Caesar dressing

1 Tbsp. lime juice

½ tsp. garlic powder

Pinch of paprika

Romaine lettuce

Toppings: cheese, tomatoes, veggies

Ingredients

3–4 boneless, skinless chicken breasts

1 chicken bouillon cube

1 C. boiling water

1 1¼-oz. env. taco seasoning mix, divided

Taco salad ingredients—tortillas, lettuce, olives, tomatoes, salsa, sour cream, cheese, etc.

SHREDDED CHICKEN TACO SALAD

1. Place chicken in bottom of slow-cooker.

2. Dissolve bouillon cube in boiling water. Once bouillon is dissolved, pour ½ of taco seasoning mix into bouillon and stir until dissolved.

3. Sprinkle other ½ of taco seasoning mix over chicken, then pour bouillon over chicken.

4. Cover and cook on LOW for 3–5 hours.

5. Drain liquid; using two forks, shred chicken. Serve chicken with taco salad ingredients.

Makes 4 servings.

COCONUT THAI SHRIMP AND RICE

1. In slow-cooker, mix the broth, water, coriander, cumin, salt, cayenne, lime zest, lime juice, garlic, and ginger.

2. Stir in the onion, bell pepper, carrot, coconut, raisins, and rice.

3. Cover and cook on LOW for 3½ hours or until rice is tender.

4. Stir in the shrimp and snow peas.

5. Cover and cook an additional 30 minutes.

6. Serve garnished with toasted coconut.

Makes 6–8 servings.

Ingredients

2 10¾-oz. cans chicken broth

1 C. water

1 tsp. ground coriander

1 tsp. ground cumin

1 tsp. salt

½–¾ tsp. cayenne pepper

Grated zest and juice of 2 limes (about ⅓ C. lime juice)

7 garlic cloves, minced

1 tsp. fresh minced ginger

1 medium onion, chopped

1 red bell pepper, diced

1 carrot, peeled and shredded

¼ C. flaked coconut

½ C. golden raisins

2 C. converted white rice

1 lb. peeled and deveined, cooked jumbo shrimp, thawed if frozen

2 oz. fresh snow peas, cut into thin strips

Toasted coconut, for garnish

SOUPS/STEWS/CHILI

Nothing is better on a chilly day than a warm bowl of soup. Serve your favorite stew, chili, or soup with crusty bread, and you've got a perfect winter meal to warm you up.

chowder
soothing
broccoli cheese
steaming
tomato basil Tortilla potato
savory medley
broth beans
Chicken noodle
comfort
lentil
roast beef stew taco soup

Ingredients

1 chicken carcass

1 carrot, chopped into large pieces

1 stalk of celery, chopped into large pieces

1 bay leaf

1 onion, quartered

Pinch of thyme

Pinch of basil

CHICKEN BROTH

1. Place the chicken carcass in the slow-cooker along with all remaining ingredients.

3. Fill the slow-cooker with water until it is ¾ full.

4. Cover and cook on LOW for 10 hours or on HIGH for 5 hours.

5. Add salt to taste, if desired.

6. Let cool in the slow-cooker. Strain out the vegetables and bones and discard.

7. Refrigerate until cold; skim off the fat. Use a measuring cup to measure out 1-cup increments; place in freezer bags. Freeze until you want to use in a recipe.

Makes 10 cups broth.

CHICKEN SOUP

1. Place chicken, onion, celery, potatoes, carrots, ketchup, and broth into slow-cooker.

2. Cover and cook on LOW for 4 hours.

3. Stir in the thyme and pepper. Cook on HIGH for 1 additional hour.

Makes 4 servings.

Ingredients

1 lb. boneless, skinless chicken thighs, cut into bite-size pieces

½ medium onion, finely chopped

2 celery ribs, finely chopped

2 medium potatoes, peeled, cubed

2 carrots, shredded or finely diced

1 Tbsp. ketchup

2 C. chicken broth

½ tsp. dried thyme

¼ tsp. black pepper

CREAMY WILD RICE AND CHICKEN SOUP

1. Combine broth, water, carrots, celery, chicken, and Rice-a-Roni® (with seasoning packet) in a large slow-cooker.

2. Cover and cook on LOW for 4–6 hours.

3. Remove chicken from slow-cooker; using two forks, shred. Return to slow-cooker.

4. In a small bowl, combine salt, pepper, and flour. In a medium saucepan, melt butter over medium heat. Stir in flour mixture, 1 Tbsp. at a time, to form a roux. Whisk in milk, a little at a time, until fully incorporated and smooth.

5. Stir roux mixture into slow-cooker; cook on LOW for an additional 15 minutes.

Makes 8 servings.

Ingredients

4 C. chicken broth

2 C. water

1 C. grated carrots

1 C. diced celery

1½ lb. boneless, skinless chicken breasts

1 pkg. Rice-a-Roni® Long-Grain & Wild Rice

½ tsp. salt

½ tsp. pepper

¾ C. all-purpose flour

½ C. butter

2 C. milk

Ingredients

1 10¾-oz. can chicken broth

1 large red potato, cubed

½ small onion, chopped

1 celery stalk, chopped

1 carrot, peeled and diced

1 Tbsp. butter

¼ tsp. black pepper

¾ lb. boneless, skinless chicken
   thighs, trimmed of fat and
   cubed

⅔ C. chopped fresh broccoli

1 Tbsp. water

⅔ C. whole milk

1 tsp. salt

½ tsp. cumin

CHICKEN & VEGETABLE MEDLEY SOUP

1. Combine broth, potato, onion, celery, carrot, butter, pepper, and chicken thighs in slow-cooker.

2. Cover and cook on LOW for 6–8 hours or on HIGH for 3–4 hours.

3. In a microwave-safe dish, cook broccoli in water for 4–5 minutes, until softened. Drain and add to slow-cooker.

4. Stir in whole milk, salt, and cumin.

5. Cover and cook for an additional 30 minutes.

Makes 4 servings.

Ingredients

1½ lb. beef stew meat

1 medium onion, chopped

1 Tbsp. olive oil

5 medium carrots, thinly sliced

4 medium red potatoes, diced

2 celery ribs, diced

2 14½-oz. cans diced tomatoes,
   undrained

2 10¾-oz. cans beef broth

1 10¾-oz. can condensed tomato soup,
   undiluted

1 Tbsp. sugar

2 tsp. Italian seasoning

1 tsp. dried parsley flakes

ALL-DAY SOUP

1. In a large skillet, brown beef and onion in oil; drain. Transfer to slow-cooker.

2. Stir in carrots, potatoes, celery, tomatoes, beef broth, tomato soup, sugar, Italian seasoning, and parsley flakes.

3. Cover and cook on LOW for 6–8 hours or until meat is tender. Stir in additional Italian seasoning and parsley to taste and cook for another 30 minutes.

Makes 8 servings.

Ingredients

1½ lb. stew meat

1 Tbsp. dehydrated onion or ¼ C. fresh chopped onion

1 carrot, finely chopped

1 celery stalk, finely chopped

1 bay leaf

2 russet potatoes, peeled and cubed

1 butternut squash, peeled and cubed (use about the same amount as the potatoes)

1 10¾-oz. can tomato soup

1 C. beef broth

1 garlic clove, minced

½ tsp. Italian seasoning

¼ tsp. black pepper

½ tsp. dried parsley flakes

¼ tsp. salt

1 tsp. quick-cooking tapioca

BEEF AND SQUASH STEW

1. Combine meat, onion, carrot, celery, bay leaf, potatoes, squash, soup, broth and garlic in slow-cooker.

2. Cover and cook on LOW for 6–8 hours.

3. Stir in the Italian seasoning, pepper, parsley flakes, salt, and tapioca.

4. Cover and cook for on LOW for an additional 30 minutes. Serve with warm bread.

Makes 4–6 servings.

PORK AND SWEET POTATO STEW

1. Place the sweet potatoes, apricots, apples, onion, and tomatoes in the bottom of slow-cooker.

2. Sprinkle with thyme; add the bay leaf and cinnamon stick.

3. Top with the pork; pour the apple juice and chicken broth over the other ingredients.

4. Cover and cook on LOW for 6–8 hours.

5. Salt and pepper to taste; serve.

Makes 6 servings.

Ingredients

3 large sweet potatoes, peeled and cubed

10 dried apricots, halved

2 apples, cored and chopped

1 onion, chopped

1 8-oz. can tomatoes

1 tsp. dried thyme

1 dried bay leaf

1 cinnamon stick

1-lb. lean boneless pork shoulder, cut into 1-inch cubes

Salt and pepper to taste

1 C. apple juice

1 C. chicken broth

Ingredients

2 lb. beef stew meat

4 celery ribs, sliced

6 carrots, shredded

6 potatoes, cubed

1 onion, chopped

1 28-oz. can diced tomatoes, undrained

¼ C. quick-cooking tapioca

1 garlic clove, pressed or minced

1 tsp. salt

¼ tsp. pepper

½ tsp. dried basil

SLOW-COOKER STEW

1. Combine beef, celery, carrots, potatoes, onion, tomatoes, tapioca, garlic, and salt in slow-cooker.

2. Cover and cook on LOW for 6–8 hours.

3. Stir in pepper and basil; serve.

Makes 6–8 servings.

Ingredients

1 lb. beef stew meat or 1-lb. chuck roast cut into small, bite-size pieces

2 carrots, finely chopped

2–3 potatoes, peeled and cubed

3 celery stalks, finely sliced

2 Tbsp. dehydrated onion or ½ C. chopped onion

1 tsp. salt

1 tsp. sugar

⅔ C. water

1 10¾-oz. can tomato soup

2 Tbsp. dry tapioca

NO-PEEK STEW

1. Combine all ingredients in slow-cooker.

2. Cover and cook on LOW for 6–8 hours or until beef is very tender.

3. Serve with freshly baked bread.

Makes 4 servings.

LEFTOVER ROAST BEEF STEW

1. Put potatoes, onion, garlic, carrots, tomatoes, broth, tomato sauce, and beef in a large slow-cooker.

2. Cover and cook on LOW for 5–6 hours.

3. Stir in the parsley flakes, Italian seasoning, seasoned salt, and pepper. Cook for 1 additional hour.

4. Salt and pepper to taste and serve.

Makes 8 servings.

Ingredients

6 potatoes, peeled and cubed

¼ C. chopped dehydrated onion or ¾ C. fresh chopped onion

2 garlic cloves, minced

¼ C. diced dehydrated carrots or ¾ C. chopped fresh carrots

1 14½-oz. can diced tomatoes, undrained

3 C. beef broth

1 8-oz. can tomato sauce

1–2 lb. leftover cooked roast beef

1 tsp. dried parsley flakes

1 tsp. Italian seasoning

1 tsp. seasoned salt

½ tsp. pepper

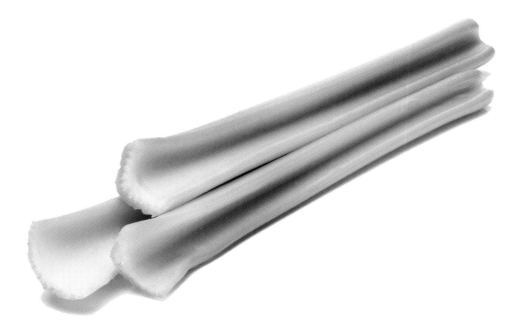

Ingredients

1 C. dried kidney beans

¼ tsp. black pepper

1 tsp. chicken bouillon granules

2 garlic cloves, minced

½ tsp. garlic salt

1 bay leaf

2 Tbsp. dried minced onion (or ½ C. chopped fresh onion)

¼ C. freeze-dried diced red bell pepper (or ½ C. fresh diced red bell pepper)

½ tsp. liquid smoke

5 C. water

1 C. wild rice

½ tsp. Cajun spice

1 Tbsp. parsley flakes

1 tsp. salt

1 lb. ground sausage, browned & drained

Red wine vinegar to taste

RED BEANS AND RICE STEW

1. Rinse beans and soak them overnight in plenty of water. They will more than double in size, so make sure there is enough water covering them.

2. Drain the beans and place in slow-cooker.

3. Add pepper, bouillon, garlic, garlic salt, bay leaf, onion, red bell pepper, liquid smoke, 5 C. water, and rice; stir to combine.

4. Cover and cook on LOW for 6 hours or on HIGH for 3 hours.

5. Stir in the Cajun spice, parsley flakes, salt, and sausage.

6. Stir in red wine vinegar to taste.

7. Cover and cook on HIGH for an additional 30–60 minutes; serve.

Makes 6 servings.

BEEF AND BARLEY SOUP

1. In a microwave-safe bowl, combine oil, onion, tomato paste, and thyme; cook for 1 minute, stir, and then cook for 1 more minute. Pour into slow-cooker.

2. Stir in vinegar, tomatoes, broths, carrot, soy sauce, barley, and roast.

3. Cover and cook on LOW for 6–8 hours, until beef is tender and barley is cooked.

4. Stir in parsley and salt and pepper to taste; serve.

Makes 3–4 servings.

Ingredients

1 Tbsp. canola oil

1 onion, minced

2 Tbsp. tomato paste

½ tsp. dried thyme

2 Tbsp. red wine vinegar

1 14-oz. can diced tomatoes, undrained

1 C. beef broth

1 C. chicken broth

1 carrot, peeled and diced

3 Tbsp. soy sauce

½ C. pearl barley

1-lb. boneless beef chuck roast, cut into 1-inch cubes

1 Tbsp. dried parsley

Salt and pepper to taste

BARLEY MUSHROOM LENTIL SOUP

1. In the slow-cooker, dissolve the bouillon cubes in the water.

2. Stir in mushrooms, barley, lentils, onion flakes, bay leaves, and garlic.

3. Cover and cook on LOW for 5–7 hours, until barley and lentils are tender.

4. Stir in thyme, sage, basil, pepper, and salt. Cover and cook on LOW for 1 additional hour.

5. Remove bay leaves and serve.

Makes 8 servings.

Ingredients

5 beef or vegetable bouillon cubes

9 C. water

4 C. sliced fresh mushrooms

¾ C. uncooked barley

¾ C. dried lentils

¼ C. dried onion flakes

3 bay leaves

3 garlic cloves, minced

1 tsp. thyme

¼ tsp. sage

1 tsp. dried basil

½ tsp. pepper, salt to taste

CREAMY MUSHROOM SOUP

1. Set aside about ½ C. of the mushrooms. Place remaining mushrooms, broth, onion, and garlic in slow-cooker.

2. Cover and cook on LOW for 4–6 hours.

3. In a small bowl, whisk sour cream, milk, cornstarch, and flour. Pour into slow-cooker. Whisk to blend with ingredients in slow-cooker. Stir in thyme, salt, and pepper.

4. Pour contents of slow-cooker into a blender or food processor. Blend until creamy.

5. Pour into bowls and top with the remaining chopped mushrooms.

Makes 4 servings.

1 16-oz. pkg. fresh button mushrooms, chopped

2 C. chicken broth

1 Tbsp. dehydrated onion

2 garlic cloves, minced

¾ C. sour cream

¾ C. milk

1 Tbsp. cornstarch

2 Tbsp. flour

⅛ tsp. dried thyme

½ tsp. salt

¼ tsp. pepper

Ingredients

cook's FAV.

2 frozen boneless, skinless chicken breast halves

3 thawed boneless, skinless chicken thighs, trimmed

1 C. chicken broth

½ C. picante sauce or salsa

1 14½-oz. can diced tomatoes in tomato juice

1 tsp. lime juice

2 garlic cloves, minced

1 10¾-oz. can cream of chicken soup

½ C. chopped red bell pepper (optional)

1–2 tsp. cumin

1 14-oz. can black beans, rinsed and drained (optional)

½ C. chopped fresh cilantro, or as much as desired

1 C. frozen corn

Tortilla chips

Grated cheese

Sour cream

CREAMY TORTILLA SOUP

1. Place chicken, broth, salsa, tomatoes, lime juice, garlic, cream of chicken soup, red pepper, 1 tsp. cumin, and black beans in slow-cooker.

2. Cover and cook on LOW for 5–7 hours.

3. Remove chicken; using two forks, shred the chicken. Put the chicken back in the slow-cooker and add extra cumin (if desired), cilantro, and corn. Cover and cook for an additional 30 minutes.

4. Serve with tortilla chips, cheese, and sour cream.

Makes 4–6 servings.

CHICKEN TORTILLA SOUP

1. In large slow-cooker, combine all ingredients except chips, cheese, and sour cream.

2. Cover and cook on LOW for 5–7 hours.

3. Just before serving, remove chicken breasts; using two forks, shred the chicken. Stir into soup.

4. To serve, put a handful of chips in each individual soup bowl. Ladle soup over chips. Top with cheese and sour cream.

Makes 6–8 servings.

Ingredients

4 uncooked boneless, skinless chicken breast halves

2 15-oz. cans black beans, rinsed and drained

2 15-oz. cans Mexican stewed tomatoes

1 C. salsa

1 4-oz. can chopped green chilies, undrained

1 14½-oz. can tomato sauce

1 14-oz. can corn, drained

½ env. taco seasoning mix (0.75 oz.)

Baked tortilla chips

Grated cheese

Sour cream

VEGETABLE TACO SOUP

1. Combine all ingredients in slow-cooker and stir to blend.

2. Cover and cook on LOW for 4 hours or until soup is heated through and flavors are blended.

3. Serve with tortilla chips or corn chips, shredded cheese, and sour cream.

Makes 5–6 servings.

Ingredients

1 lb. lean ground beef, browned

1 10¾-oz. can vegetable soup

1 10¾-oz. can tomato soup

1 16-oz. can kidney beans, rinsed and drained

2 14-oz. cans diced tomatoes, undrained

1 C. salsa

1 Tbsp. chili powder

1 Tbsp. taco seasoning

Ingredients

1 lb. ground beef, browned, drained

1 1¼-oz. env. taco seasoning

1 14-oz. can corn

1 14-oz. can kidney beans, pinto beans, or black beans

2 8-oz. cans tomato sauce

1 14½-oz. can diced tomatoes

TACO SOUP

1. Combine all ingredients in slow-cooker and stir to blend.

2. Cover and cook on LOW for 4–6 hours.

3. Serve with corn chips, cheese, and sour cream.

Makes 4-6 servings.

Ingredients

1 lb. 95% lean ground chicken, browned

1 14½-oz. can Great Northern beans, rinsed and drained

1 16-oz. can chicken broth

2 garlic cloves, minced

½ tsp. salt

1 Tbsp. lime juice

1 bay leaf

1 4-oz. can diced green chilies

1 14½-oz. can diced tomatoes

1 tsp. oregano

¼ tsp. ground red pepper

2 C. frozen corn

Cilantro, cheese, and sour cream

HEALTHY CHICKEN FIESTA SOUP

1. Add chicken, beans, broth, garlic, salt, lime juice, bay leaf, green chilies, and tomatoes to slow-cooker.

2. Cover and cook on LOW for 4–6 hours.

3. Stir in oregano, ground red pepper, and corn. Cover and cook for an additional 30 minutes.

4. Ladle into bowls and serve with cilantro, cheese, and sour cream, if desired.

Makes 6 servings.

NACHO CHEESE SOUP

1. Place chicken, broth, salsa, tomatoes, lime juice, garlic, soup, red bell pepper, cumin, and green chilies in slow-cooker.

2. Cover and cook on LOW for 6–8 hours.

3. Stir in cilantro, corn, and beans. Salt and pepper to taste. Add more cumin and lime juice if needed.

4. Cover and cook for an additional 30 minutes.

5. Serve with tortilla chips, cheese, and sour cream.

Makes 6 servings.

Ingredients

2 boneless, skinless chicken breast halves (can be frozen)

2 boneless, skinless chicken thighs

1 C. chicken broth

½ C. salsa

1 14½-oz. can diced tomatoes

1 tsp. lime juice

2 garlic cloves

1 10¾-oz. can Campbell's® Fiesta Nacho Cheese Soup

½ C. chopped red bell pepper (optional)

1 tsp. cumin

1 4-oz. can diced green chilies

½ C. chopped fresh cilantro, or as much as desired

1 C. frozen corn

1 14-oz. can black or pinto beans, rinsed and drained (optional)

Salt and pepper to taste

Tortilla chips

Grated cheese

Sour cream

Ingredients

2 14-oz. cans diced tomatoes, undrained

1 C. finely diced celery

1 C. finely diced carrots

4 C. chicken broth

1 C. finely diced onions

1 tsp. dried oregano or 1 Tbsp. fresh oregano

1 Tbsp. dried basil or ¼ C. fresh basil

½ bay leaf

½ C. butter

½ C. flour

1 C. Parmesan cheese

2 C. half-and-half, warmed

1 tsp. salt

¼ tsp. black pepper

TOMATO BASIL PARMESAN SOUP

1. Combine tomatoes, celery, carrots, chicken broth, onions, fresh oregano, fresh basil, and bay leaf in a large slow-cooker. (If using dried oregano and basil, add them in the last hour of cooking time.)

2. Cover and cook on LOW for 5–7 hours, until flavors are blended and vegetables are soft.

3. About an hour before serving prepare a roux. In a large skillet, melt butter over low heat; stir in flour. Stir constantly with a whisk for 5–7 minutes. Slowly stir in 1 C. hot soup. Add another 3 C. hot soup and stir until smooth. Pour the roux-soup combination back into the slow-cooker.

4. Add the Parmesan cheese, warmed half-and-half, salt, and pepper; stir well. If using dried oregano and basil, add them now. Cover and cook on LOW for 1 additional hour until ready to serve.

Makes 8 servings.

Ingredients

2 lb. red potatoes, peeled and cut into ½-inch cubes

¾ C. finely chopped carrots

1 medium onion, finely chopped

3 C. chicken broth

½ tsp. salt

1 C. whole milk

¼ tsp. black pepper

2 C. shredded Cheddar cheese

EASY CHEESY POTATO SOUP

1. Place potatoes, carrots, onion, broth, and salt in slow-cooker.

2. Cover and cook on LOW for 4–6 hours.

3. Stir in milk and pepper.

4. Cover; cook on HIGH for 15 minutes.

5. Turn off slow-cooker. Stir in cheese; stir until melted. Serve.

Makes 6 servings.

Ingredients

2 lb. red potatoes, peeled and cut into ½-inch cubes

¾ C. grated carrots

3 Tbsp. dehydrated onions or ½ C. finely chopped fresh onions

3 C. chicken broth

½ tsp. salt

1 C. warmed whole milk

¼ tsp. black pepper

½ C. freeze-dried broccoli or 1 C. blanched fresh broccoli florets

2 C. shredded medium or sharp cheddar cheese

BROCCOLI CHEESE SOUP

1. Place potatoes, carrots, onions, broth, and salt in slow-cooker.

2. Cover and cook on LOW for 4–6 hours.

3. Stir in warmed milk, pepper, broccoli, and cheese. Cover and cook on HIGH for 15 minutes or until cheese is melted and broccoli is soft.

Makes 6 servings.

TOMATO RAVIOLI SOUP

1. In a skillet, melt butter. Add tomatoes, onions, brown sugar, tomato paste, and salt; cook over medium heat for about 5 minutes. Stir in the flour and cook 1 minute longer. Whisk in 1 C. broth. Transfer contents of skillet to the slow-cooker.

2. Stir in remaining broth, reserved tomato juice, and bay leaves.

3. Cover and cook on LOW for 4–6 hours.

4. Discard the bay leaves.

5. Pour contents of slow-cooker into a food processor or blender. Blend until smooth. Pour back into the slow-cooker.

6. Stir in the milk, basil, and ravioli. Cover and cook on HIGH for 1 additional hour, or until ravioli are cooked through.

7. Salt and pepper to taste and serve.

Makes 6–8 servings.

Ingredients

2 Tbsp. butter

3 14½-oz. cans diced tomatoes, drained, juice reserved

1 small onion, diced finely

1 Tbsp. brown sugar

1 Tbsp. tomato paste

½ tsp. salt

2 Tbsp. flour

3 C. chicken broth, divided

2 bay leaves

½ C. evaporated milk

1½ tsp. dried basil or 1 Tbsp. fresh basil

12 oz. frozen ravioli

ITALIAN TORTELLINI SOUP

1. In a skillet, brown sausage, onion, and garlic; drain grease. Transfer to slow-cooker.

2. Add broth, water, tomatoes, carrots, and tomato sauce to slow-cooker.

3. Cover and cook on LOW for 5–7 hours.

4. Stir in basil, oregano, zucchini, green pepper, and frozen tortellini.

5. Cover and cook on HIGH for 1 additional hour or until tortellini is done.

Makes 8 servings.

Ingredients

1 lb. mild bulk Italian sausage

1 C. chopped onion

2 garlic cloves, minced

5 C. beef broth

1 C. water

1 14-oz. can diced tomatoes

1 C. grated carrots

1 8-oz. can tomato sauce

½ tsp. basil

½ tsp. oregano

1½ C. shredded zucchini

1 medium green pepper, chopped

8 oz. frozen tortellini

Ingredients

1 lb. bulk Italian sausage, browned
and drained

2 cans chicken broth

1 C. water

1 garlic clove, minced

3 large russet potatoes, cubed

¼ C. onion, finely diced

Bacon bits to taste

1 C. heavy cream

1 bunch fresh kale, coarsely chopped

Grated Parmesan cheese, for garnish

Ingredients

1 onion, minced

4 garlic cloves, minced

1 Tbsp. olive oil

1 Tbsp. chili powder

½ tsp. dried oregano

5 C. chicken broth

3 medium red potatoes, cubed

5 pieces crispy cooked bacon,
crumbled

8 oz. kielbasa sausage, sliced into
½-inch slices

8 oz. kale, stems removed, leaves
sliced ¼-inch thick

1 5-oz. can evaporated milk, warmed

½ C. Parmesan cheese

Salt and pepper to taste

ZUPPA TOSCANA

1. Place Italian sausage, chicken broth, water, garlic, potatoes, and onion in slow-cooker.

2. Cover and cook on LOW for 6–8 hours or on HIGH for 3–4 hours, until potatoes are cooked and soft.

3. Add bacon bits, cream, and kale right before serving.

4. Top with Parmesan cheese and serve with fresh bread.

Makes 8 servings.

KIELBASA AND KALE SOUP

1. In a microwave-safe dish, combine onion, garlic, oil, chili powder, and oregano; cook for 3–4 minutes, stirring every minute. Transfer to a slow-cooker.

2. Add broth, potatoes, bacon, and kielbasa.

3. Cover and cook on LOW for 4–6 hours.

4. Stir in the kale, warmed evaporated milk, and Parmesan cheese. Whisk to blend.

5. Cook on HIGH for an additional 20 minutes.

6. Season with salt and pepper and serve.

Makes 6 servings.

PASTA FAGIOLI SOUP

1. In a large skillet, brown beef; drain. Add onion and garlic; sauté until onion is transparent, then transfer to a large slow-cooker.

2. Add carrots, celery, tomatoes, red and white beans, broth, and spaghetti sauce to slow-cooker.

3. Cover and cook on LOW for 4–7 hours or on HIGH for 2–4 hours.

4. During last 1 hour on LOW or last 30 minutes on HIGH, stir in pasta, oregano, pepper, parsley, and Tabasco sauce (if desired).

5. Serve with grated Parmesan cheese on top.

Makes 8–10 servings.

Ingredients

2 lb. ground beef

1 onion, chopped

3 garlic cloves, minced

3 carrots, chopped

3 ribs of celery, chopped

2 28-oz. cans diced tomatoes with juice

1 16-oz. can red kidney beans, rinsed and drained

1 16-oz. can white kidney beans, rinsed and drained

3 10¾-oz. cans beef broth

1 26-oz. jar spaghetti sauce

8 oz. rotini pasta, cooked and drained

3 tsp. oregano

2 tsp. pepper

5 tsp. parsley flakes

1 tsp. Tabasco sauce (optional)

Grated Parmesan cheese, for garnish

CLAM CHOWDER

1. In a skillet, fry bacon until crispy; drain on paper towels and crumble when cool.

2. In the same skillet, cook onion until clear. Place onion and crumbled bacon in slow-cooker.

3. Stir in clams (with the juice), water, potatoes, celery, and corn.

4. Cover and cook on LOW for 4–6 hours.

5. In a saucepan, combine the butter, milk, half-and-half, and flour; cook on low and whisk until the roux is thick and bubbly.

6. Mix ½ C. of the liquid from the slow-cooker into the roux. Then add the roux to the slow-cooker and stir to blend well.

7. Salt and pepper to taste.

8. Cover and cook on LOW for an additional 30 minutes.

Makes 8 servings.

CREAMY CORN CHOWDER

1. In slow-cooker, combine chicken, corn, soup, chili peppers, cilantro, taco seasoning, and black beans. Stir in broth.

2. Cover and cook on LOW for 5–6 hours.

3. In a medium bowl, stir about 1 C. of the hot soup into the sour cream. Stir sour cream mixture and cream cheese into the soup in the slow-cooker; cover and let stand 5 minutes. Stir with a whisk until combined.

4. Garnish with cilantro and serve.

Makes 8 servings.

Ingredients

¼ lb. bacon

1 large onion, chopped

2 cans minced clams, undrained

½ C. water

2–3 large potatoes, peeled and cubed

3 celery stalks, finely chopped

1 11-oz. can corn, drained

Salt and pepper to taste

2 Tbsp. butter

1 C. milk

1 C. half-and-half

½ C. flour

Salt and pepper to taste

Ingredients

1 lb. boneless, skinless chicken breasts, cut into ½-inch pieces

1 11-oz. can whole-kernel corn with sweet peppers, drained

1 10¾-oz. can condensed cream of potato soup

1 4-oz. can diced green chili peppers

2 Tbsp. snipped fresh cilantro plus extra for garnish

1 1¼-oz. env. taco seasoning

1 14-oz. can black beans, rinsed and drained

2 C. chicken broth

8 oz. sour cream

4 oz. cream cheese

Ingredients

3 C. chicken broth

1½ C. water

¾ tsp. coriander

¾ tsp. cumin

½ C. lime juice

3 garlic cloves, minced

¼ C. flaked coconut

1½ Tbsp. fresh grated ginger

1 medium onion, finely diced

1 red bell pepper, diced

1 carrot, finely chopped or shredded

1 14-oz. can coconut milk, divided

4 boneless, skinless chicken thighs, trimmed of fat and cubed

1 C. chopped fresh mushrooms

½ tsp. salt

½ tsp. pepper

Cumin, salt, and pepper to taste

LIME COCONUT SOUP

1. Combine broth, water, coriander, cumin, lime juice, garlic, flaked coconut, ginger, onion, red bell pepper, carrot, 7 oz. coconut milk, chicken, mushrooms, salt, and pepper in the slow-cooker.

2. Cover and cook on LOW for 4–6 hours.

3. Stir in the rest of the coconut milk. Add cumin, salt, and pepper to taste; serve.

Makes 8 servings.

COCONUT THAI SOUP

1. In a microwave-safe bowl, combine onions, garlic, ginger, and oil; cook for about 4 minutes until onions are softened. Transfer to slow-cooker.

2. Stir in broth, ½ the can of coconut milk, lemon grass, carrot, ½ Tbsp. fish sauce, cilantro stems, and chicken.

3. Cover and cook on LOW for 4–6 hours, until chicken is tender.

4. Remove the chicken from the slow-cooker; using two forks, shred the chicken into bite-size pieces. Return to slow-cooker.

5. Let soup settle; skim off fat from the surface.

6. Discard the lemon grass and cilantro stems.

7. Stir in the mushrooms, warmed remaining coconut milk, 1 Tbsp. fish sauce, lime juice, sugar, and curry paste.

8. Season with salt and pepper and garnish with cilantro; serve.

Makes 4 servings.

Ingredients

1 onion, minced

3 garlic cloves, minced

1 Tbsp. grated fresh ginger

1½ tsp. canola oil

2 C. chicken broth

1 14-oz. can coconut milk, divided

1 stalk lemon grass (trim off bottom 5 inches, peel off outer layer, and smash the stalk with the back of a chef's knife)

1 grated carrot

1½ Tbsp. fish sauce, divided

10 cilantro stems, tied together, plus extra for garnish

2 boneless, skinless chicken thighs, trimmed of fat

4 oz. white mushrooms, sliced

2 Tbsp. lime juice

2 tsp. sugar

1 tsp. Thai red curry paste

Salt and pepper to taste

Ingredients

1 lb. mixed dry beans

6 C. water

Ham bone

1½ C. ham, cubed

1 large onion, chopped

¾ C. celery, chopped

¾ C. carrots, sliced or chopped

1 15-oz. can diced tomatoes

2 Tbsp. fresh parsley, chopped

1 C. tomato juice

2 Tbsp. Worcestershire sauce

1 bay leaf

1 tsp. prepared mustard

½ tsp. chili powder

Juice of 1 lemon

1 tsp. salt

½ tsp. black pepper

HAM AND BEAN SOUP

1. Place beans in saucepan; cover with 6 C. water and soak overnight.

2. Drain the liquid.

3. Combine beans and remaining ingredients in slow-cooker.

4. Cover and cook on LOW for 7–9 hours.

5. Salt and pepper to taste. Remove bay leaf and ham bone before serving.

Makes 10 servings.

HAM & POTATO SOUP

1. Spray slow-cooker with nonstick cooking spray.

2. Layer potatoes, ham, and beans in slow-cooker.

3. In medium bowl, combine soup, water, and cheese. Pour over potatoes and ham.

4. Cover and cook on LOW for 6–8 hours or on HIGH for 3–4 hours, or until potatoes are very tender.

5. Stir soup and serve.

Makes 6 servings.

Ingredients

6 large russet potatoes, peeled and cubed

1 lb. ham, cubed

1 16-oz. can Great Northern beans, rinsed and drained

1 10¾-oz. can cream of mushroom soup

1 C. water

½ C. shredded cheddar cheese

BLACK BEAN CHILI

1. Rinse the black beans and place in the slow-cooker. Add 4 C. water.

2. Cover and cook on HIGH for 2½–3½ hours, until beans are soft. Drain the liquid.

3. Stir in remaining ingredients.

4. Cover and cook on HIGH for an additional 2–3 hours.

4. Serve with sour cream and corn chips, if desired.

Makes 4–6 servings.

Ingredients

1 C. dry black beans

4 C. water

1 lb. lean ground beef, cooked and drained

¼ C. dried onion

1 8-oz. can tomato sauce

1 14-oz. can diced tomatoes, drained

2 Tbsp. lime juice

½ tsp. garlic salt

2 tsp. chili powder

2 tsp. cumin

½ tsp. cinnamon

Ingredients

1 onion, minced

½ env. taco seasoning mix (0.5 oz.)

1 Tbsp. tomato paste

1 Tbsp. canola oil

3 garlic cloves, minced

1 15-oz. can black beans, drained, rinsed

1 8-oz. can tomato sauce

1 14½-oz. can diced tomatoes

1 tsp. brown sugar

½–1 lb. leftover meatloaf or 1 lb. lean ground beef, browned & drained

1 C. frozen corn

Grated cheese

Sour cream

Tortilla or corn chips

TACO CHILI

1. In a microwave-safe dish, combine onions, taco seasoning mix, tomato paste, oil, and garlic; cook for 3–4 minutes, stirring every minute. Pour onion mixture into slow-cooker.

2. Stir in the beans, tomato sauce, tomatoes, and brown sugar.

3. Crumble the meatloaf (or cooked ground beef) and stir into the slow-cooker.

4. Cover and cook on LOW for 4–6 hours.

5. Stir in the frozen corn.

6. Top each serving with cheese, sour cream, and tortilla or corn chips.

Makes 4 servings.

Ingredients

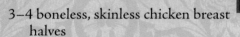

3–4 boneless, skinless chicken breast halves

2 10¾-oz. cans chicken broth

2 tsp. ground cumin

2 tsp. dried oregano

3 garlic cloves, minced

1 tsp. salt

½ tsp. red pepper flakes

2 16-oz. cans Great Northern beans

1 16-oz. can white shoepeg corn

2 Tbsp. chopped fresh cilantro

3 Tbsp. lime juice

WHITE CHILI

1. Add chicken, broth, cumin, oregano, garlic, salt, and red pepper to slow-cooker.

2. Cover and let cook on LOW for 5–7 hours or until chicken falls apart.

3. Remove the chicken from the slow-cooker. Using two forks, shred the chicken; return to the slow-cooker.

4. Drain and rinse the beans and corn and add them to the slow-cooker.

5. Stir in chopped cilantro and lime juice.

6. Cover and let cook for an additional 30 minutes, until heated through.

Makes 6 servings.

LIME CHICKEN CHILI

1. In a medium bowl, use a fork to mash bread and milk into a paste. Mix in the ground chicken, salt, and pepper.

2. In a skillet, heat oil; stir in the onions, chili powder, tomato paste, garlic, cumin, oregano, and red pepper. Cook until onions are softened, about 5 minutes. Stir in the chicken mixture and cook for about 3 minutes. Stir in the tomato sauce; transfer contents to slow-cooker.

3. Add the diced tomatoes, beans, soy sauce, and honey.

4. Cover and cook on LOW for 4–6 hours.

5. Stir in lime juice and salt and pepper to taste; serve.

Makes 6 servings.

Ingredients

1 slice whole-wheat bread

2 Tbsp. milk

1 lb. ground chicken

¼ tsp. salt

¼ tsp. pepper

1 Tbsp. canola oil

1 small onion, finely diced

1 Tbsp. chili powder

2 Tbsp. tomato paste

3 garlic cloves, minced

2 tsp. ground cumin

½ tsp. dried oregano

⅛ tsp. ground red pepper

1 8-oz. can tomato sauce

¼ C. salsa

1 14½-oz. can diced tomatoes, with juice

1 15-oz. can pinto beans, drained and rinsed

2 Tbsp. soy sauce

1 Tbsp. honey

1 Tbsp. lime juice

DESSERTS

Dessert in the slow-cooker? Yes—yes, you can. Free up oven space by baking your cobbler in the slow-cooker, and you'll have the added benefit of an appealing aroma drifting through your home for hours!

peanut butter

pudding Brownies

baked delight cake

cream Sweet

crumble

Sauce cookie

apple crisp fondue

caramel

chocolate

Ingredients

3 large fresh peaches, peeled and sliced, or frozen sliced peaches

⅓ C. flour

⅓ C. quick-cooking oats

⅓ C. brown sugar

½ tsp. cinnamon

Dash of nutmeg

¼ C. butter

Vanilla ice cream

PEACH CRISP

1. Place sliced peaches in bottom of slow-cooker.

2. In a medium bowl, combine the flour, oats, brown sugar, cinnamon, and nutmeg. Cut the butter in with a pastry blender or a fork. Mixture should be crumbly. Sprinkle over the peaches.

3. Cover the slow-cooker with a paper towel. Put the lid over the paper towel to seal the slow-cooker.

4. Cook on HIGH for 2 hours.

5. Serve warm with vanilla ice cream.

Makes 4–5 servings.

Ingredients

1¾ C. sugar

1 C. canola oil

2 eggs

1 tsp. vanilla

2 C. chopped apples

2 C. flour

1 tsp. salt

1 tsp. baking soda

1 tsp. nutmeg

APPLE CAKE

1. In a large bowl, beat sugar, oil, and eggs until smooth. Add vanilla and apples. Mix well.

2. In a separate bowl, sift flour, salt, baking soda, and nutmeg. Stir flour mixture into apple mixture until well blended.

3. Pour batter into greased and floured bread or cake pan that fits into slow-cooker.

4. Cover pan loosely with greased tin foil. Place pan in slow-cooker.

5. Cover and cook on HIGH for 2–4 hours.

6. Let cake stand in pan for 5 minutes after removing from slow-cooker. Remove cake from pan, slice, and serve.

Makes 6 servings.

APPLE CRISP

1. Place sliced apples in slow-cooker.

2. In a medium bowl, combine oats, flour, brown sugar, cinnamon, and nutmeg. Cut in softened butter until mixture is crumbly. Sprinkle over apples.

3. Cover the top of the slow-cooker with 2 paper towels. Place the slow-cooker lid on top of the paper towels to seal the slow-cooker.

4. Cover and cook on HIGH for 2–3 hours.

5. Serve with vanilla ice cream.

Makes 8 servings.

Ingredients

2 lb. cooking apples, peeled and sliced (about 6 medium apples)

⅔ C. old-fashioned oats

⅔ C. flour

⅔ C. packed light brown sugar

¾ tsp. cinnamon

¼ tsp. ground nutmeg

½ C. butter, softened

Vanilla ice cream

APPLE PEANUT CRUMBLE

1. Place apple slices in slow-cooker.

2. In a medium bowl, combine brown sugar, flour, oats, cinnamon, and nutmeg. Cut in butter and peanut butter. Sprinkle over apples.

3. Cover the top of the slow-cooker with 2 paper towels. Place the slow-cooker lid on top of the paper towels to seal the slow-cooker.

4. Cover and cook on HIGH for 2–3 hours.

5. Serve warm or cold, plain or with ice cream or whipped cream.

Makes 4–5 servings.

Ingredients

4–5 cooking apples, peeled and sliced

⅔ C. packed brown sugar

½ C. flour

½ C. quick-cooking oats

½ tsp. cinnamon

¼ tsp. nutmeg

⅓ C. butter, softened

2 Tbsp. peanut butter

Ice cream or whipped cream (optional)

Ingredients

4 very large tart apples, cored

½ C. apple juice

8 Tbsp. brown sugar

12 hot cinnamon candies

4 Tbsp. butter

8 caramel candies

¼ tsp. ground cinnamon

Vanilla ice cream (optional)

Ingredients

4 large baking apples

1 Tbsp. lemon juice

⅓ C. chopped dried apricots

⅓ C. chopped walnuts or pecans

3 Tbsp. packed brown sugar

½ tsp. ground cinnamon

2 Tbsp. melted butter

½ C. water

Caramel ice cream topping (optional)

CARAMEL APPLES

1. Place each apple on a piece of foil; wrap the foil around the apple so the filing can't escape.

2. Place apples in bottom of slow-cooker.

3. Pour apple juice over apples.

4. Fill the center of each apple with 2 Tbsp. brown sugar, 3 hot cinnamon candies, 1 Tbsp. butter, and 2 caramel candies. Sprinkle with cinnamon.

5. Cover and cook on LOW for 4–6 hours or on HIGH for 2–3 hours, or until tender.

6. Serve hot with ice cream, if desired.

Makes 4 servings.

FRUIT AND NUT BAKED APPLES

1. Scoop out center of each apple, leaving a 1½-inch-wide cavity about ½ inch from the bottom.

2. Peel top of each apple down about 1 inch. Brush peeled edges evenly with lemon juice.

3. In a small bowl, mix apricots, nuts, brown sugar, and cinnamon. Add butter; mix well. Spoon mixture evenly into apple cavities.

4. Pour ½ C. water onto bottom of slow-cooker. Place apples in slow-cooker.

5. Cover and cook on LOW for 3–4 hours or on HIGH for 2 hours.

6. Serve warm or at room temperature with caramel ice cream topping, if desired.

Makes 4–6 servings.

SPICED APPLESAUCE

1. Place apples in slow-cooker.

2. In a small bowl, combine sugar and cinnamon. Mix with apples.

3. Stir in water, lemon juice, and nutmeg.

4. Cover and cook on LOW for 5–7 hours or on HIGH for 2½–3½ hours.

5. For a chunky applesauce, stir with a wire whisk; for pureed applesauce, blend in a food processor.

6. Serve hot or cold.

Makes 6 cups applesauce.

12 C. peeled, cored, and thinly sliced cooking apples

½ C. sugar

½ tsp. cinnamon

1 C. water

1 Tbsp. lemon juice

Fresh grated nutmeg, optional

Ingredients

8 apples, peeled, cored, and cut into small chunks (about 6 C.)

1 tsp. cinnamon

½ C. water

½ C. sugar

Ingredients

3 C. water

1 C. sugar

10 slices fresh ginger

2 whole cinnamon sticks

6 Bartlett pears, peeled and cored

CHUNKY APPLESAUCE

1. Combine all ingredients in slow-cooker.

2. Cover and cook on LOW for 6–8 hours or on HIGH for 3–4 hours.

3. Serve hot or cold.

Makes 8–10 servings.

CINNAMON-GINGER POACHED PEARS

1. Combine water, sugar, ginger, and cinnamon sticks in slow-cooker. Add pears.

2. Cover and cook on LOW for 4–6 hours or on HIGH for 1½–2 hours.

3. Remove pears from slow-cooker.

4. Continue cooking liquid in slow-cooker, uncovered, 30 minutes or until thickened.

5. Drizzle pears with syrup and serve.

Makes 6 servings.

LOW-FAT CARROT CAKE

1. Turn slow-cooker to HIGH. Spray with nonfat cooking spray.

2. In a medium bowl with mixer on medium speed, beat the egg whites, sour cream, applesauce, cinnamon, and cake mix for 2 minutes, scraping the sides of the bowl occasionally. With spatula, stir the carrots into the batter until well mixed. Pour the prepared batter into the slow-cooker.

3. Place a paper towel on top of the slow-cooker; place the slow-cooker lid on top of the paper towel to seal. Cover and cook on HIGH for 1½–2 hours or until knife inserted in center comes out clean.

4. Remove the insert from the slow-cooker. Remove lid and paper towel, and let the cake cool for 10–15 minutes.

5. Run a knife around the outside edge of the cake to loosen.

6. Place a large serving plate upside down on top of the slow-cooker. Holding the slow-cooker and the plate firmly together, carefully flip the cake upside down. It will be steamy hot, so be careful.

7. Serve hot or chilled with vanilla ice cream.

Makes 8–10 servings.

Ingredients

6 egg whites

½ C. nonfat sour cream

½ C. applesauce

1 tsp. ground cinnamon

1 20-oz. box carrot cake mix

3 C. carrots, finely shredded

Vanilla ice cream

THAT'S GOOD PEACHES

1. Spray slow-cooker with nonstick cooking spray.

2. In a large bowl, combine the Bisquick®, oatmeal, cinnamon, and sugars. Fold in the peaches and pour into the slow-cooker.

3. Cover and cook on HIGH for 2 hours or on LOW for 3–4 hours.

4. Serve with whipped cream or vanilla ice cream.

Makes 4 servings.

Ingredients

4 C. sliced fresh or frozen peaches

⅓ C. Bisquick®

⅔ C. oatmeal

¼ tsp. cinnamon

½ C. sugar

½ C. brown sugar

Whipped cream or vanilla ice cream

Ingredients

1 21-oz. can cherry pie filling

2 C. all-purpose flour

½ C. sugar

½ C. butter, melted

1 C. milk

1 Tbsp. baking powder

1 tsp. almond extract

½ tsp. salt

CHERRY COBBLER

1. Spray slow-cooker with nonstick cooking spray. Pour pie filling into slow-cooker.

2. In a medium bowl, beat remaining ingredients until smooth. Spread batter over pie filling.

3. Cover and cook on HIGH for 1½–2 hours or until toothpick inserted in center comes out clean.

Makes 6–8 servings.

Ingredients

1 21-oz. can cherry pie filling

1 pkg. white or yellow cake mix

½ C. butter, melted

Vanilla ice cream

2 minute prep

★ cook's FAV.

CHERRY DELIGHT

1. Spray slow-cooker with nonstick cooking spray. Pour pie filling into greased slow-cooker.

2. In a medium bowl, combine dry cake mix and butter (mixture will be crumbly). Sprinkle over filling.

3. Cover and cook on LOW for 4 hours or on HIGH for 2 hours.

4. Serve with vanilla ice cream.

Makes 6–8 servings.

Ingredients

1 C. flour

¾ C. sugar

1 tsp. baking powder

¼ tsp. salt

¼ tsp. ground cinnamon

¼ tsp. ground nutmeg

2 eggs, beaten

2 Tbsp. milk

2 Tbsp. vegetable oil

4 C. fresh or frozen blueberries

¾ C. water

1 tsp. grated orange peel

¾ C. sugar

Vanilla ice cream (optional)

Ingredients

8 C. cubed French bread, stale or toasted

¾ C. semisweet chocolate chips

½ C. canned solid-pack pumpkin

1½ C. half-and-half or heavy cream

½ C. brown sugar

3 eggs

3 Tbsp. butter, melted

½ tsp. salt

1 tsp. cinnamon

2 tsp. vanilla

BLUEBERRY COBBLER

1. In a medium bowl, combine flour, ¾ C. sugar, baking powder, salt, cinnamon, and nutmeg.

2. In a small bowl, combine eggs, milk, and oil. Stir into dry ingredients until moistened.

3. Spread the batter evenly over bottom of greased slow-cooker.

4. In a saucepan, combine blueberries, water, orange peel, and ¾ C. sugar; bring to a boil. Remove from heat and pour over batter.

5. Cover and cook on HIGH for about 3 hours, or until toothpick inserted into batter comes out clean.

6. Turn off slow-cooker and remove the cover. Let stand 30 minutes before serving. Spoon from cooker and serve with ice cream, if desired.

Makes 6 servings.

PUMPKIN CHOCOLATE CHIP BREAD PUDDING

1. Spray slow-cooker with nonstick baking spray. Place bread and chocolate chips in slow-cooker and stir gently to mix.

2. In a medium bowl, combine pumpkin with half-and-half or cream; stir. Add remaining ingredients and mix until smooth. Pour mixture into slow-cooker.

3. Push bread down into liquid if necessary.

4. Cover and cook on HIGH for 2 hours or until pudding is set. Turn off slow-cooker; remove cover. Let bread pudding stand for 15 minutes before serving.

Makes 8 servings.

PUMPKIN PUREE

1. Wash the outside of the pumpkin thoroughly.

2. Using a sharp knife, cut the pumpkin in half; using a spoon, scoop out seeds and strings.

3. Cut pumpkin into pieces small enough to fit in the slow-cooker. Fill slow-cooker with pumpkin.

4. Cover slow-cooker and turn to LOW. Check after about 3 hours and every 30–60 minutes thereafter. Pumpkin is cooked when it can be easily pierced with a fork.

5. Let pumpkin cool, then scoop it out of tough shells.

6. Process in food processor or blender until smooth; use in recipes in place of canned pumpkin.

Ingredients

1 pumpkin

Ingredients

1 16-oz. can pureed pumpkin

¾ C. sugar

½ C. flour

½ tsp. baking powder

2 eggs, beaten

2 Tbsp. butter, melted

4 oz. cream cheese, softened

1 Tbsp. pumpkin pie spice

2 tsp. vanilla

Whipped cream or vanilla ice cream

CRUSTLESS PUMPKIN CREAM CHEESE PIE

1. In a large bowl, mix all ingredients except whipped cream until smooth. Pour into greased slow-cooker.

2. Cover and cook on LOW for 3–5 hours (it will be a puddinglike consistency).

3. Serve in bowls with whipped cream or vanilla ice cream.

Makes 4–5 servings.

Ingredients

1½ C. skim milk

1 C. hot, cooked rice

3 eggs, beaten

½ C. sugar

¼ C. dried cranberries

½ tsp. almond extract

¼ tsp. salt

CRANBERRY RICE PUDDING

1. In a large bowl, combine all ingredients. Pour mixture into greased 1½-quart casserole dish and cover with foil.

2. Place rack in bottom of a 6-quart slow-cooker. Pour in 1 C. water. Place dish on the rack in the slow-cooker.

3. Cover and cook on LOW for 4–5 hours.

4. Remove dish from slow-cooker. Let stand for 15 minutes before serving.

Makes 6 servings.

CHOCOLATE BANANA BREAD PUDDING

1. In a large bowl, mix eggs, milk, sugar, and vanilla until smooth. Stir in bread, bananas, and chocolate chips; let rest 5 minutes for bread to soak.

2. Pour into greased slow-cooker.

3. Cover and cook on HIGH for 2 hours.

Makes 6 servings.

Ingredients

- 4 eggs
- 2 C. milk
- 1 C. sugar
- 1 Tbsp. vanilla extract
- 4 C. cubed French bread, stale or toasted
- 2 bananas, sliced
- 1 C. semisweet chocolate chips

NUTELLA® BREAD PUDDING

1. Spray slow-cooker with nonstick cooking spray.

2. Combine bread and chocolate chips in slow-cooker.

3. In a medium bowl, whisk half-and-half, egg yolks, Nutella, white sugar, vanilla, and salt; pour over bread in the slow-cooker. Press on bread so all is submerged in liquid. Sprinkle brown sugar over the top.

4. Cover and cook on LOW for 3 hours, until the center is set.

5. Serve with ice cream, if desired.

Makes 4–5 servings.

Ingredients

- 6–8 slices toasted French bread, cut into 1-inch cubes (about 6 C.)
- ¼ C. semisweet chocolate chips
- 2 C. half-and-half
- 4 large egg yolks
- ½ C. Nutella®
- 6 Tbsp. white sugar
- 2 tsp. vanilla extract
- ¼ tsp. salt
- 1 Tbsp. brown sugar
- Ice cream (optional)

CHOCOLATE PEANUT BUTTER BREAD PUDDING

1. Spray slow-cooker with nonstick cooking spray.

2. Toss bread cubes and chocolate chips together in slow-cooker.

3. In a medium bowl, whisk milk, egg yolks, sugar, peanut butter, vanilla, salt, and cocoa. Pour over the top of the bread, and push bread down so it is submerged in the liquid.

4. Cover and cook on LOW for 3–4 hours or on HIGH for 1½–2 hours.

Makes 6 servings.

Ingredients

6 C. cubed French bread (stale or toasted)

½ C. semisweet chocolate chips

2 C. evaporated milk

4 egg yolks

⅓ C. sugar

½ C. peanut butter

2 tsp. vanilla

¼ tsp. salt

¼ C. cocoa

HOT FUDGE PUDDING CAKE

1. In a medium bowl, mix 1 C. brown sugar, flour, 3 Tbsp. cocoa, baking powder, and salt. Stir in milk, butter, and vanilla; beat until smooth. Spread over the bottom of greased slow-cooker.

2. In a small bowl, mix ¾ C. brown sugar and ¼ C. cocoa. Sprinkle over mixture in slow-cooker.

3. Pour boiling water over batter. Do not stir.

4. Cover and cook on HIGH for 2–3 hours, or until a toothpick inserted in center comes out clean.

5. Serve sauce and cake warm with vanilla ice cream.

Makes 8 servings.

Ingredients

1 C. packed brown sugar

1 C. flour

3 Tbsp. cocoa

2 tsp. baking powder

½ tsp. salt

½ C. milk

2 Tbsp. melted butter

½ tsp. vanilla

¾ C. packed brown sugar

¼ C. cocoa

1¾ C. boiling water

Vanilla ice cream

Ingredients

1 ⅔ C. flour

¾ C. brown sugar

¼ C. unsweetened cocoa powder

½ tsp. baking soda

¼ tsp. salt

1 egg

⅓ C. water

3 Tbsp. peanut butter

2 Tbsp. butter, melted

1 tsp. vanilla

1 C. milk chocolate chips

¼ C. caramel ice-cream topping

¼ C. brown sugar

¾ C. water

3 Tbsp. cocoa mixed with 1 Tbsp. oil

½ tsp. vanilla

Ice cream or whipped cream

BROWNIE FUDGE CAKE

1. In a large bowl, combine flour, ¾ C. brown sugar, ¼ C. cocoa, baking soda, and salt; mix well.

2. In a small bowl, combine egg with ⅓ C. water, peanut butter, melted butter, and 1 tsp. vanilla; mix well.

3. Stir peanut butter mixture into flour mixture until combined. Add chocolate chips.

4. Spray slow-cooker with nonstick baking spray containing flour. Pour batter into slow-cooker.

5. In a small saucepan, combine ice-cream topping, ¼ C. brown sugar, ¾ C. water, and cocoa-oil mixture; cook and stir over medium heat until chocolate melts and mixture is smooth. Stir in ½ tsp. vanilla; pour over batter. Do not stir.

6. Cover and cook on HIGH for 2–2½ hours.

7. Turn off slow-cooker, place lid ajar, and let stand for 30 minutes. Serve with ice cream or whipped cream.

Makes 8 servings.

Ingredients

½ C. peanut butter

⅓ C. butter

⅛ tsp. vanilla

2 C. powdered sugar

1 ⅓ C. semisweet chocolate chips

BUCKEYES

1. In a large bowl, mix the peanut butter, butter, vanilla, and powdered sugar. (The dough will look dry.)

2. Roll into one-inch balls and place on a waxed paper-lined plate or cookie sheet.

3. Chill in the freezer until firm, about 30 minutes.

4. While the dough is chilling, dump the chocolate chips into slow-cooker; cover and cook on HIGH for 30 minutes. Stir until smooth.

5. Dip the firm balls into the chocolate and coat entirely, except for the very top. Put back on cookie sheet and refrigerate until serving.

Makes 10 servings.

HOT CARAMEL AND CHOCOLATE CAKE

1. In a small microwave-safe bowl, combine cream cheese and milk. Cook on 50% power for 1 minute; remove and stir. Continue cooking for 30-second intervals until cream cheese melts; stir with wire whisk to blend.

2. Place cream cheese mixture in large bowl; stir in sour cream, cocoa powder, and egg. Mix well. Add both packages of muffin mix; stir just until combined.

3. Spray slow-cooker with nonstick baking spray containing flour. Spread batter evenly in slow-cooker.

4. In small saucepan, combine butter, brown sugar, ice-cream topping, and water; heat to boiling, stirring until blended. Carefully pour over batter in slow-cooker. Do not stir.

5. Cover and cook on HIGH for 2½–3 hours or until cake springs back when lightly touched.

6. Uncover, turn off slow-cooker, top loosely with foil, and let stand for 30 minutes. Gently run a sharp knife around the edges of the cake and invert over serving plate until cake drops out. If any sauce remains in slow-cooker, spoon over cake. Cool for 30 minutes before serving.

7. Serve cake and sauce with vanilla ice cream.

Makes 8 servings.

Ingredients

4 oz. cream cheese, cubed

½ C. milk

1 C. sour cream

¼ C. unsweetened cocoa powder

1 egg

2 8.2-oz. pkgs. chocolate chip muffin mix

2 Tbsp. butter

½ C. brown sugar

½ C. caramel ice-cream topping

½ C. water

Vanilla ice cream

Ingredients

1 21½-oz. Betty Crocker® Triple Chocolate cake mix

1 pkg. (4-serving size) instant French vanilla pudding and pie filling mix

1 C. sour cream

2 C. Heath® toffee bits, divided

1 C. chocolate chips

1 C. water

¾ C. canola oil

Vanilla ice cream

HEATH® BAR CHOCOLATE PUDDING CAKE

1. Spray slow-cooker with nonstick cooking spray.

2. In a large bowl, combine cake mix, pudding mix, sour cream, 1 C. toffee bits, chocolate chips, water, and oil; stir well to combine. Batter will be slightly lumpy. Pour into slow-cooker.

3. Cover and cook on HIGH for 1½–2 hours. Middle will be a little gooey and puddinglike.

4. Top with remaining toffee bits and serve with vanilla ice cream.

Makes 10 servings.

PEANUT BUTTER & HOT FUDGE PUDDING CAKE

1. In a medium bowl, combine flour, powdered sugar, and baking powder. Stir in the milk, oil, and vanilla. Mix until smooth and then stir in peanut butter. Pour batter into greased slow-cooker.

2. Mix sugar and cocoa powder. Gradually stir boiling water into cocoa mixture. Pour over batter in slow-cooker. Do not stir.

3. Cover and cook on HIGH for 2–3 hours or until toothpick inserted in center comes out clean.

4. Serve warm with vanilla ice cream.

Makes 8 servings.

Ingredients

½ C. flour

¼ C. powdered sugar

¾ tsp. baking powder

⅓ C. milk

1 Tbsp. oil

½ tsp. vanilla

¼ C. peanut butter

½ C. sugar

3½ Tbsp. unsweetened cocoa powder

1 C. boiling water

Vanilla ice cream

PEANUTTY CHOCOLATE PUDDING CAKE

1. In a bowl, stir flour, ½ C. sugar, 2 Tbsp. cocoa, and baking powder. Add milk, oil, and vanilla; stir batter until smooth. Stir in the peanut butter chips. Spread batter evenly in the bottom of greased slow-cooker.

2. In a bowl, combine ¾ C. sugar and ¼ C. cocoa. In a separate bowl, combine boiling water and peanut butter; stir into the cocoa mixture. Pour evenly over the batter in the slow-cooker. Do not stir.

3. Cover and cook on HIGH for 2–3 hours.

4. Let stand, uncovered, for 30 minutes to cool slightly. Spoon pudding cake into dessert dishes. Sprinkle with peanuts. Serve with vanilla ice cream.

Makes 8 servings.

Ingredients

1 C. all-purpose flour

½ C. sugar

2 Tbsp. cocoa powder

1½ tsp. baking powder

½ C. milk

2 Tbsp. vegetable oil

1 tsp. vanilla

¾ C. peanut butter-flavored chips

¾ C. sugar

¼ C. cocoa powder

2 C. boiling water

½ C. chunky peanut butter

2 Tbsp. chopped peanuts

Vanilla ice cream

Ingredients

3 Tbsp. unsalted butter

2 oz. semisweet chocolate

6 Tbsp. sugar

1 Tbsp. cornstarch

1 egg

1 egg yolk

Vanilla ice cream

CHOCOLATE SOUFFLÉ

1. In a saucepan over low heat, melt the butter and chocolate. Set aside.

2. In a mixing bowl, combine the sugar and cornstarch.

3. In a separate bowl, whisk the egg and the egg yolk.

4. Combine the melted butter-chocolate mixture and the sugar mixture; combine thoroughly with a wire whisk. Stir in the eggs and whisk just until smooth.

5. Scoop the mixture into 3 ramekins; each should be ⅔ full. Place ramekins on top of a rack inside the slow-cooker.

6. Cover and cook on HIGH for 1–1½ hours. Center will not be set.

7. Serve immediately with vanilla ice cream.

Makes 3 servings.

Ingredients

1 21½-oz. box chocolate cake mix

1 8-oz. container sour cream

1 pkg. (4-serving size) instant chocolate pudding mix

1 C. chocolate chips

¾ C. canola oil

4 eggs

1 C. water

TRIPLE CHOCOLATE SURPRISE

1. Spray slow-cooker with nonstick cooking spray. In a large bowl, mix all ingredients by hand. Pour into slow-cooker.

2. Cover and cook on HIGH for 2–3 hours.

3. Serve hot or warm with ice cream or whipped cream.

Makes 10 servings.

Ingredients

1 C. unsalted butter, at room temperature

2 eggs

½ C. firmly packed brown sugar

½ C. white sugar

1 Tbsp. pure vanilla extract

2 C. all-purpose flour

½ tsp. baking soda

¼ tsp. salt

1½ C. semisweet chocolate chips

CHOCOLATE CHIP COOKIE BARS

1. Spray slow-cooker with nonstick cooking spray. Cut a piece of waxed paper to fit the bottom and grease the waxed paper.

2. In a bowl, beat the butter, eggs, sugars, and vanilla until light and fluffy.

3. In a separate bowl, stir the flour, baking soda, and salt. Stir the dry ingredients into the butter mixture. Fold in the chocolate chips until well blended.

3. Spoon the dough evenly into the slow-cooker and smooth the top.

4. Cover and cook on LOW for about 3 hours, until a toothpick inserted into the center comes out clean.

5. Set the lid slightly ajar. Turn off the heat and remove the insert from the slow-cooker. Allow to cool in the insert for 30 minutes. Invert onto a wire rack; cut and serve.

Makes 6–8 servings.

BROWNIE HALLOWEEN SURPRISE

1. Fill each of 6 oven-safe ramekins with about 1½ Tbsp. of brownie batter.

2. Place a piece of Halloween candy on top of batter in each ramekin; spoon another 2 Tbsp. batter on top of candy until the candy is completely covered.

3. Place a rack in the bottom of a large oval slow-cooker (if you don't have a rack, use crumpled-up balls of foil). Place ramekins on top of rack or foil so that air can circulate under them.

4. Cover and cook on HIGH for 2 hours.

5. Serve with vanilla ice cream.

Makes 6 servings.

Ingredients

1 brownie mix, prepared according to package directions

Leftover Halloween candy

Vanilla ice cream

OREO™ CREAM CHEESE BROWNIES

1. Following the directions on the brownie mix box, make the brownie batter.

2. In a small bowl, mix the cream cheese and Oreo™ crumbs.

3. Mix the cream cheese mixture and the brownie batter.

4. Pour into a greased oval slow-cooker. Place a thick paper towel on top of the slow-cooker; cover the paper towel with the lid so it is tightly sealed. Cook on HIGH for 2 hours, until toothpick inserted in the center comes out clean.

5. Serve with vanilla ice cream.

Makes 8–10 servings.

Ingredients

1 brownie mix

4 oz. cream cheese, softened

10 Oreos™, crushed into crumbs

Vanilla ice cream

Ingredients

1 20-oz. Ghiradelli Double
   Chocolate brownie mix

Caramel topping

4 oz. cream cheese

2 C. frozen or fresh raspberries,
   divided

Vanilla ice cream

CARAMEL RASPBERRY CREAM CHEESE BROWNIES

1. Place a small rack or trivet in the bottom of a large slow-cooker. If you don't have a rack, you can ball up pieces of foil to hold the dish off the bottom of the slow-cooker.

2. Spray an oven-safe dish that fits in your slow-cooker with nonstick cooking spray.

3. Make the brownie mix according to directions on the box. Pour the brownie batter into the dish until it's about ⅔ full (you'll probably have extra batter).

4. Plop 2–4 Tbsp. of the caramel topping in dollops on top of the brownie batter; don't mix in.

5. Soften the cream cheese in the microwave on 50% power for 30 seconds. Plop dollops of the cream cheese on top of the batter.

6. Using the tip of a knife, lightly score the top surface to slightly mix the cream cheese and caramel into the batter. It should look marbled.

7. Sprinkle 1 C. raspberries on top of the batter. Push down on the raspberries slightly.

8. Place a large paper towel on top of the slow-cooker. Cover the slow-cooker with the lid. Cook on HIGH for 1½–2½ hours.

9. Serve with extra raspberries on top and vanilla ice cream on the side.

Makes 16 servings.

SLOW-COOKER BROWNIES

1. Spray oval slow-cooker with cooking spray.

2. In a small bowl, whisk flour and baking powder; set aside.

3. In the microwave or on the stovetop, combine and melt butter and chocolate chips. Whisk in ⅔ C. sugar, 3 Tbsp. cocoa, vanilla, salt, milk, and egg yolk. Add flour mixture and mix thoroughly. Pour into slow-cooker and spread evenly.

4. In a medium bowl, whisk remaining sugar, cocoa, brown sugar, and hot water until sugar is dissolved; slowly pour over batter in slow-cooker.

5. Cover and cook on HIGH for 1½–2½ hours. The moist brownie will pull away from the sides and will float on a layer of molten chocolate.

6. Let cool for 25 minutes; serve with whipped cream or vanilla ice cream.

Makes 8–10 servings.

Ingredients

1 C. flour
2 tsp. baking powder
6 Tbsp. butter
⅓ C. semisweet chocolate chips
⅔ plus ⅓ C. sugar
3 Tbsp. plus ⅓ C. cocoa
1 Tbsp. vanilla
¼ tsp. salt
⅓ C. milk
1 egg yolk
⅓ C. brown sugar
1½ C. hot water
Whipped cream or vanilla ice cream

CREAM CHEESE BROWNIES

1. In a medium bowl, beat butter, 1 C. sugar, and 1 egg until well blended. Stir in flour, salt, cocoa, and ½ tsp. vanilla. Pour into greased slow-cooker.

2. In a small bowl with a mixer at low speed, beat cream cheese, ¼ C. sugar, 1 egg, and ½ tsp. vanilla until just mixed. Beat for 2 minutes at medium speed. Drop dollops of cream cheese mixture on top of batter. Using the tip of a knife, lightly score the top surface to mix the cream cheese mixture in slightly.

3. Cover and cook on HIGH for 2 hours, until toothpick inserted in center comes out clean.

Makes 8 servings.

Ingredients

½ C. butter, melted
1¼ C. sugar, divided
2 eggs, divided
½ C. flour
¼ tsp. salt
2 Tbsp. cocoa
1 tsp. vanilla, divided
4 oz. cream cheese, softened

Ingredients

1 C. butter

2 C. sugar

4 eggs, room temperature

1½ tsp. vanilla

Zest from 1 orange

3 C. flour, divided

1 tsp. baking powder

½ tsp. salt

1 12-oz. pkg. fresh cranberries

Glaze: 2 Tbsp. orange juice and 1 C. powdered sugar

CRANBERRY ORANGE CAKE

1. In a large bowl, use a mixer to cream butter and sugar. Add eggs, one at a time, vanilla, and orange zest.

2. In a separate bowl, sift 2¾ C. flour, baking powder, and salt. Blend with creamed mixture.

3. Fold in remaining ¼ C. flour and the cranberries.

4. Cut waxed or parchment paper in an oval shape to fit 6-quart oval slow-cooker; put in bottom of slow-cooker. Pour batter into slow-cooker. Cover and cook on HIGH for 3 hours, until toothpick inserted in the middle comes out clean.

5. When cool, place large oval plate on top of slow-cooker insert. Flip over slow-cooker so that the cake comes out onto the plate. Remove waxed paper.

6. Make glaze by whisking the orange juice and powdered sugar until smooth. Drizzle glaze over the top of the cake.

Makes 10 servings.

Ingredients

1 C. semisweet chocolate chips

1 C. butterscotch chips

½ C. peanut butter

5 C. corn flakes cereal

CRISPY CHOCOLATE BARS

1. Place chocolate chips, butterscotch chips, and peanut butter into slow-cooker; stir to combine.

2. Cover and cook on LOW for 1½–2 hours.

3. Remove lid and stir until smooth. Add corn flakes and stir until well coated.

4. Press cereal mixture into a greased square baking dish. Cool; cut into squares and serve.

Makes 6–8 servings.

Ingredients

2 lb. white coating chocolate, broken into small pieces

2 C. semisweet chocolate chips

1 4-oz. pkg. sweet German chocolate

1 16-oz. jar dry-roasted peanuts (salted or unsalted)

2 C. crispy rice cereal

Ingredients

1 C. semisweet chocolate chips

2 Tbsp. butter

¼ C. peanut butter

1 C. quick-cooking oats

6 Tbsp. powdered sugar

½ tsp. vanilla

EASY CHOCOLATE CLUSTERS

1. Combine all ingredients except peanuts and cereal in slow-cooker.

2. Cover and cook on HIGH for 1 hour.

3. Stir and reduce heat to LOW; cook 1 additional hour, or until chocolate is melted, stirring every 15 minutes. Stir in peanuts and cereal and mix well.

4. Pour into greased 9 x 13 dish and pat down. Let cool. Cut and eat.

Makes 10–12 servings.

NO-BAKE COOKIES

1. Combine chocolate chips, butter, and peanut butter in slow-cooker.

2. Cover and cook on HIGH for 1 hour.

3. Stir in oats, powdered sugar, and vanilla. Drop by spoonfuls onto waxed paper.

4. Let cool and serve.

Makes 10–15 servings.

FUDGY GRAHAM COOKIES

1. Place chocolate chips and cocoa mixture in large slow-cooker.

2. Cover and cook on HIGH for 1 hour, stirring every 15 minutes.

3. Continue to cook on LOW heat for 30 minutes, stirring every 15 minutes.

4. Stir milk into melted chocolate.

5. Add 3 C. graham cracker crumbs, 1 C. at a time, stirring after each addition. Stir in nuts. Mixture should be thick but not stiff. Stir in remaining graham cracker crumbs until mixture is consistency of cookie dough.

6. Drop by heaping teaspoonfuls onto lightly greased cookie sheets. Keep remaining mixture warm by covering and turning the slow-cooker to warm.

7. Bake in preheated oven at 325 degrees for 7–9 minutes, or until tops of cookies begin to crack. Remove from oven. Cool 1–2 minutes before transferring to waxed paper.

Makes 8 dozen cookies.

Ingredients

- 1 12-oz. pkg. semisweet chocolate chips
- 6 Tbsp. cocoa powder mixed with 2 Tbsp. oil
- 2 14-oz. cans sweetened condensed milk
- 3¾ C. crushed graham cracker crumbs
- 1 C. finely chopped walnuts

SEVEN-LAYER BARS

1. In a bread pan or cake pan that fits into the bottom of a large slow-cooker, layer the butter, crumbs, chocolate chips, peanut butter chips, coconut, and walnuts; drizzle the sweetened condensed milk over the top. Do not stir.

2. Cover and bake on HIGH for 2–3 hours, or until firm.

3. Remove pan and uncover. Let stand 5 minutes. Cut and serve.

Makes 6–8 servings.

Ingredients

- ¼ C. melted butter
- ½ C. graham cracker crumbs
- ½ C. chocolate chips
- ½ C. peanut butter chips
- ½ C. flaked coconut
- ½ C. chopped walnuts
- ½ C. sweetened condensed milk

Ingredients

1 14-oz. can sweetened condensed milk

½ C. peanut butter

½ C. evaporated milk

Bananas, apples, or angel food cake

PEANUT BUTTER AND CARAMEL FONDUE

1. Peel the label off the sweetened condensed milk; place the can of milk in the slow-cooker.

2. Fill the slow-cooker insert with water until it covers the can.

3. Cover and cook on LOW for 8 hours or on HIGH for 4 hours.

4. Remove can from slow-cooker and let rest.

5. Drain water out of the slow-cooker.

6. Add peanut butter to slow-cooker; stir in cooled sweetened condensed milk.

7. Slowly add evaporated milk, whisking until smooth.

8. Turn slow-cooker to warm and serve with bananas, apples, or angel food cake.

Makes 8 servings.

Ingredients

1 C. semisweet chocolate chips

6–9 oz. evaporated milk (depending how thick you want the sauce)

½ C. creamy peanut butter

2 minute prep

PEANUT BUTTER HOT FUDGE SAUCE

1. Combine all ingredients in slow-cooker.

2. Cover and cook on HIGH for 30–60 minutes.

3. Stir until creamy and serve over ice cream.

Makes 10–15 servings.

SYMPHONY® BAR FONDUE

1. Break up candy bars and place in slow-cooker. Add cream.

2. Cover and cook on HIGH for 1–2 hours. Stir until creamy.

2. Turn slow-cooker to warm and dip pieces of banana, apple, marshmallow, angel food cake, or pretzels into chocolate.

Makes 10–15 servings.

Ingredients

3 large Symphony® milk chocolate bars with nuts and toffee bits (about 12 oz. total)

1 C. heavy cream

Bananas, apples, marshmallows, angel food cake, and/or pretzels

CHOCOLATE PEANUT BUTTER NUT FONDUE

1. Combine all ingredients in slow-cooker; stir.

2. Cover and cook on HIGH for 1 hour.

3. Stir and turn to warm setting. Dip fruit, cake, or marshmallows in fondue.

Makes 10–15 servings.

Ingredients

1 12-oz. bag semisweet chocolate chips

1 C. powdered sugar

1 C. chunky peanut butter

1 12-oz. can evaporated milk

Fruit, cake, or marshmallows

WITCHES' HATS

1. Set aside 1¾ C. M&Ms®.

2. Using a rolling pin, crush remaining M&Ms®. Combine crushed M&Ms®, milk, and butter in slow-cooker.

3. Cover and cook on HIGH for 1 hour. Stir until smooth. Cool to room temperature.

4. Frost top of each cookie with 1½ Tbsp. M&Ms® mixture.

5. Frost cones with M&M® mixture, leaving 1 inch at tip unfrosted.

6. Holding frosted cone by tip, fill each cone with 2 Tbsp. M&Ms®.

7. Center an upside-down filled cone on top of each frosted cookie to form a witch's hat. Place each hat on baking sheet.

8. Repeat until all cookies and cones are used.

9. Decorate with remaining M&Ms®.

Makes 12 servings.

Ingredients

4 C. M&Ms®, divided

⅓ C. evaporated milk

3 Tbsp. butter

12 3-inch chocolate cookies

12 sugar ice cream cones

Ingredients

¾ C. sugar

½ C. unsalted butter

½ C. heavy cream

¼ C. light corn syrup

Dash of salt

½ C. semisweet chocolate chips

¾ C. cocoa mixed with ¼ C. melted butter or oil

2 tsp. pure vanilla extract

KILLER DARK CHOCOLATE SAUCE

1. Combine sugar, butter, cream, corn syrup, and salt in the slow-cooker.

2. Cover and cook on LOW for 1½ hours.

3. Stir with a whisk until smooth; sugar must be dissolved.

4. Stir in chocolate chips, cocoa mixture, and vanilla extract.

5. Cover and continue to cook on LOW for an additional 30–60 minutes.

6. Stir until smooth. Serve warm over ice cream.

Makes about 2 cups of sauce.

Ingredients

1 C. semisweet chocolate chips

½ C. evaporated milk

½ tsp. vanilla

⅓ C. powdered sugar

2 C. frozen raspberries, divided

Ice cream

2 minute prep

RASPBERRY CHOCOLATE SAUCE

1. Place chocolate chips, evaporated milk, vanilla, and powdered sugar in slow-cooker.

2. Cover and cook on LOW for 1–2 hours.

3. Stir and then toss in 1 C. raspberries. Add more evaporated milk if needed.

3. Serve over ice cream and top with remaining raspberries.

Makes 3 cups sauce.

CARAMEL SAUCE

1. Remove label from milk can.

2. Place unopened can on side in a slow-cooker. Fill insert with water until it is 3–4 inches above can.

3. Cover and cook on LOW for 8 hours or on HIGH for 4 hours.

4. Turn off slow-cooker and allow can to cool for 40 minutes inside slow-cooker.

5. Chill caramel in unopened can in refrigerator until ready to serve.

6. Use as a dip for apple slices or serve over ice cream.

Makes 8–10 servings.

2
minute
prep

**ALL
DAY**

★
cook's
FAV.

Ingredients

1 14-oz. can sweetened condensed
  milk

Water

INDEX